AF168247

YOUR PRESENCE IS

A DANGER TO YOUR LIFE

Samar Yazbek, born in 1970, is a Syrian writer and journalist. A prominent advocate for human and women's rights, she took part in the 2011 popular uprising against the Assad regime and was forced into exile soon after. She was named one of the Beirut39 most promising authors under the age of forty in 2010 and was awarded the PEN Pinter Prize International Writer of Courage Award in 2012, followed by the Swedish Tucholsky Prize and the Dutch Oxfam/ PEN Prize. In 2022, she was selected as one of twelve International Writers by the Royal Society of Literature. Yazbek has published two collections of short stories, seven novels and four non-fiction literary narratives, and has been translated into over twenty languages.

Leri Price is an award-winning literary translator of contemporary Arabic fiction. She has been a Finalist for the National Book Award for Translated Literature three times: in 2024 for her translation of Samar Yazbek's *Where the Wind Calls Home*; in 2021 for her translation of Samar Yazbek's *Planet of Clay*; and in 2019 for Khaled Khalifa's *Death is Hard Work*, which also won the 2020 Saif Ghobash-Banipal Prize for Arabic Literary Translation.

'This is a remarkable, shattering book that holds its voices with dignity and care. It speaks to us from a red world of absolute loss, yet is suffused with an extraordinary persistence of love. Beyond geopolitics, rhetoric, territory and leaders, there remains the bare fact of broken lives and the unbearable weight of human love.'
— A. L. Kennedy, author of *Alive in the Merciful Country*

'Since the start of Israel's genocide against Palestinians, I have been grasping for words. Yazbek has done something extraordinary. She has captured the vocabulary we have all been searching for by turning to the people who witnessed this violence first hand in Gaza. The book does not make heroes of genocide survivors, nor does it romanticize their struggle. Instead, we are invited to mourn with them, to marvel at their endurance, and to be sobered by humanity's capacity for barbarism. Yazbek shows us what it means to bear witness, to make space for grief, pain and suffering too vast to be contained, and how to do so with dignity, respect and humility. She has once again modelled what it means to be a keeper of humanity's memory.'
— Tareq Baconi, author of *Fire in Every Direction*

'These testimonies of the unconscionably injured are among hundreds of thousands such testimonies emerging from Gaza since 7 October 2023. Despite Israel's genocidal drive to silence Palestinian voices, despite Western complicity in this silencing, these twenty-six testimonies – shared with Yazbek and translated by Price – now exist as pages. If, like me, you have the means and the capacity to read them in all their blistering detail, and if you too have no personal knowledge of the unspeakable zannanat that plague these pages, then you – we – have a particular duty: not only to read these precious words, but to act on them.'
— Natasha Soobramanien, co-author (with Luke Williams) of *Diego Garcia*

Fitzcarraldo Editions

YOUR PRESENCE IS
A DANGER TO YOUR LIFE

VOICES FROM GAZA

SAMAR YAZBEK

Translated by
LERI PRICE

These testimonies were collected by the author between March and June 2024.

MEDITERRANEAN SEA

DEIR AL-BALAH

AL-AQSA
HOSP.

AL-RASHID ROAD

NASSER HOSP.

AL-AMAL HOSP.

KHAN YOUNIS

EUROPEAN
HOSP.

RAFAH

AL-NAJJAR HOSP.

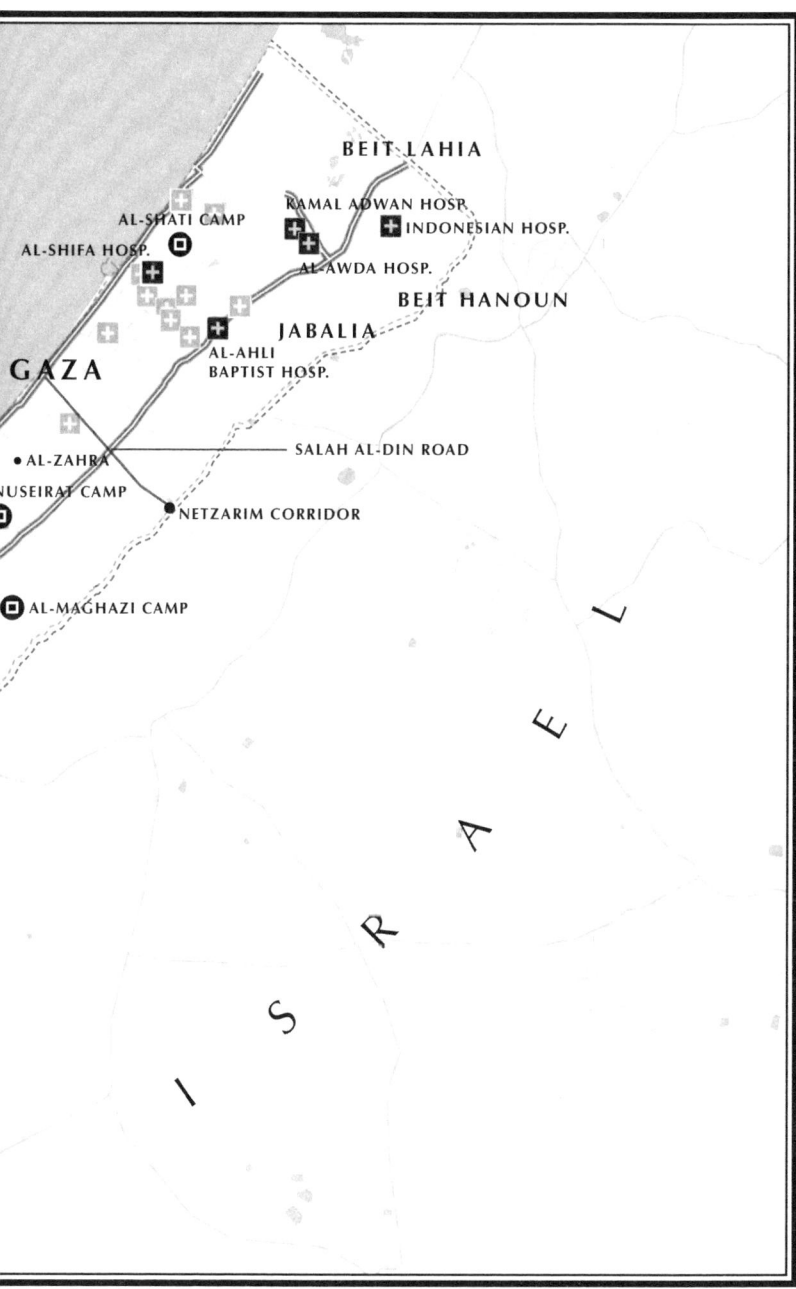

BEIT LAHIA

KAMAL ADWAN HOSP.

INDONESIAN HOSP.

AL-SHATI CAMP

AL-SHIFA HOSP.

AL-AWDA HOSP.

BEIT HANOUN

JABALIA

AL-AHLI
BAPTIST HOSP.

GAZA

• AL-ZAHRA

SALAH AL-DIN ROAD

NUSEIRAT CAMP

• NETZARIM CORRIDOR

AL-MAGHAZI CAMP

ISRAEL

INTRODUCTION

It is noon. I pause, resisting the haziness of vision that transforms the stone buildings into white arms trembling in the breeze, then continue moving along the wide avenue, trying to seek shelter from the burning midday sun. A few seconds later, I open my eyes as wide as they can go. I stare at the end of the street where black silhouettes are coming closer, moving oddly, shapes with uncertain features that blur and vanish into the mirage as if flying. I try and bring them into focus, struggling to grasp what is happening at the end of this unfamiliar road.

At the time, I wasn't very familiar with this place. The map of the area was an enigma, and my sense of what was happening there was confused. I found myself, as intended, at a government office in Thumama. There, survivors of the Gazan genocide were gathered; people with amputated limbs in complex and critical states of health. Together with the family members caring for them, they numbered more than 2,500. This fantastical scene was taking place in a quiet city called Doha, but in those moments, the destruction in Syria was re-enacted for me. The silhouettes of the victims, the very same moans – it was disaster, all over again.

There wasn't a living soul around. The cruel, oozing midday sun was burning my forehead, and strange qualms began to wrestle me in the desert noon. I looked away at first, trying to escape the thoughts taking hold, but then took a few steps closer, trying to distinguish those black shadows, and realized they were wheelchairs being pushed by others. I turned around, only to see a woman in black pushing a chair that carried a young woman in the prime of life. It occurred to me that the whole world had come to this: missing body parts, people with amputated limbs, half-bodies living on the margins of life like remnants of a bygone age. I felt like we were on board a ship hovering in mid-air, suspended within a destiny of impotence and loss, among delusions and ghosts I couldn't quite make out. The sun was pitiless, and I had to head to the administrative offices to meet some officials. A train of thought transformed what I was seeing into an image from a novel, an attempt to maintain my equilibrium in the face of this reality. And to drive from my mind the interwoven scenes of ruin, the confusion between which was Syria and which Palestine.

A strange grief nearly swallowed up the spectacle, as if the place was rendered unreal by the excess of its tragedy. Who can bear such agony?

It was no coincidence that I saw the devastation conveyed by these wheelchairs, so like flocks of black birds and carrying the resounding suffering of the Palestinian people – a people plucked out by the root and left to dangle in limitless space. Those phantoms embodied a recurring symbol of humanity's defeat, as if Palestinians had become Syrians and Syrians Palestinians, across a shared space of brutality that I have witnessed, written about and buried in my heart.

I found myself facing those wheelchairs and the people who had survived the torments of genocide, impelled to try and understand their pain. I felt called upon as a writer trading in words and narrative as a means of empathy, of effecting change and, most crucially, of understanding the dangerous world around us, thinking of a better, more humane future. I was still panting in the wake of these racing thoughts, still drawn towards these people by the ideas so deeply rooted within me. These people meant a great deal to me. One way or another, Syria was before me at that moment and, as always, I held fast to the imperative of not leaving the victims alone, the imperative of movement and action and feeling; these are the conditions of our existence, and by necessity our humanity.

I was stuck, suddenly, by a searing question – what happened to the people of Gaza who survived the genocide? Is it even right that we consider them survivors? Where does human pain go when justice is absent? How did they lose parts of their bodies and embark on new forms of existence? How can we deal with their sufferings? How can it be that the lives of ordinary people, having dwelled for years in an open prison, have vanished forever since that infamous day, 7 October? There is something else in the speed of this disappearance – destruction and a redoubled, unfathomable barbarity have settled over these people. Why do we drone on and on about their issues in political and ideological slogans, far removed from their subjective, individual pain?

These questions were troubling, but I did my best to collect myself that desert afternoon as I walked towards them. I said a greeting, and received some weak smiles and diffident glances in reply. Instantly, I realized that I was going to stay here. I was going to live among them, try to grasp the details of their lives and sit by their side with their grief – the grief that has made me come to recognize them as heroes and honourable people who resist so as to stay alive.

Why have I come back to writing about war? Once again, memory returns, more insistent than ever.

Between doubt and certainty lies the narrative of truth. We must approach language's shadows and ghosts, we must listen to the voices of the victims. Now, precisely, language needs to bend beneath this rope pulled taut over our souls, a rope which overwhelms the mind's capacity to fathom the curses that have settled over our countries.

What should we do with these terrifying stories? Can the language of silence provide a way out of these desperate circumstances? Between blood-smeared facts, it is perhaps language's transformation into silence that reveals our periodic failure to approximate atrocities. Yes; humans are capable of brutalizing each other, in ways that challenge language's very capacity of expression.

For years, I have been attempting and thinking of new ways to rewrite and reinforce stories of the people and places we have come from. It is an attempt at reconstruction, extending beyond literature and documentation to reveal a different narrative, one that explores the pain and overwhelming catastrophe in our world. Now more than ever, this devastation writes our world in its own way: in pictures and numbers which erase it from humanity's collective conscience, turning it into a momentary consumer product and causing fundamental meanings to disappear within the fetid decay of the immediate moment.

And so, we find ourselves adrift in the face of the transformations that genocidal wars impose on meaning and language, after the destruction of people. We are the offspring of war and tragedy, discussing horrors and humanity's ability to destroy the world through sheer evil. On the other hand, we also possess the capacity to see the moment of destruction, to face it and work to overcome it, even from within catastrophe itself. There are those who no longer see any meaning to life, of course. And there are those who now concentrate the meaning of their lives on the memory of those who have left them, the loved ones who are so greatly missed. Violence can be neither described nor believed, to the point that we are powerless to narrate it. But these survivors are here; despite everything, they are living, in every sense of the word – with their questions, with their wish to understand what

14

has happened to them, with their inability to understand. They are people who have passed through hell and returned.

How can I enquire into the act of erasing people, of erasing stone? The narration of genocide relies fundamentally on this act, and erasure is in itself one of the forms of its permanence, its power and consummation – in the sense of its dominance, in the sense of our inability to communicate with it. This erasure is apparent in every aspect of genocide: the erasure of dismembered bodies; the erasure of our ability to see clearly; the erasure of the profound act of bearing witness to the agony of others; the erasure of language. Erasure here is absolute, and we can only think of it as a primary material in the reassemblage of these scattered bodies.

Everything and its inverse can be found within accounts of the catastrophes that devour the human body, and to which we happen to be witnesses; these contradictions all form part of the story of evil as told throughout history. It is the narrative of moments articulated out of survivors' remembrances of destruction. I have carried out similar work in previous books: *Woman in the Crossfire*, *The Crossing* and *Nineteen Women*. Here, I do not speak about my novels, but my various narrative undertakings to construct the shattered world.

In the current, terrible circumstances of war in Gaza, I thought about testimonies of the moment of 7 October, an interrogation of that period as it slid towards ruin, beginning with the instant the world flipped over and showed another face. There is a question, often repeated among both male and female survivors of intentional, methodical genocide. This question finds expression through persistence of repetition, but also contains its own negation, in the sense that forming this question, reflecting

15

on it, only nullifies it. If I could be more specific, then writing about these outrages would no longer demand imaginative, creative writing as much as it would search within direct narrative writing which attempts to gather the limbs of truth scattered here and there, venerating the personal and the subjective by turning stories of erasure into narrative.

Life consists of a collection of experiences, and the same thing applies, if not more so, to violence. When these experiences of exceptional violence are not gathered together in a cohesive story, they evade us. Just as the limbs scattered in Gaza testify to the annihilation of the body, the absence of a narration of violence *as it is lived on a personal level* accomplishes the annihilation of people. Like the Palestinians who desperately strive to collect the scattered parts of their loved ones in order to reconstruct them, there is an urgent need to collect a large number of stories and experiences that will survive this slaughter, and which will lay bare for future generations a truth of what comes from violence.

Narrative permits us, if not to understand what happened, then at least to acknowledge the agony of the victims, to acknowledge human horror in all its forms.

This narrative seeks to reassemble what has been erased, in the sense of rewriting one of the faces of truth. I personally regard this as essential; I ardently aspire to seek truth, and devote myself to becoming acquainted with its various faces. In trying to understand this violent world we live in, I find myself concerned with this different form of narrative, even though the question of truth is still occupied with undoing the erasure that is endemic in the lives of these victims.

In addressing the overwhelming and unbearable grief that confronts the question of erasure, we suppose that the context of Syria and Gaza is part of viewing people's lives as they endure catastrophe, while their lives are bound for effacement. This does not relate only to history or documentation, to furthering discussion of the roles of victims and executioners and the procurement of justice. It is a separate, challenging question, but it is part of what I am trying to think about.

How can we think about reviving the pain of others in an attempt to stop it recurring? How can we think of the future, when a person's erased life is not reassembled, in word and deed, until we think about justice for them, about filling in their outlines? We do this, perhaps, through bringing their memories to life, making them rebels against the discourses that reduce them to cumulative statistics, trying to extract their humanity from the objectification manufactured by the machinery of express consumerist media. We attempt it by turning the story of each person into a lofty edifice, in the way that a human life deserves to be an entire country; for collective memory is – in short – their story, and her story, and my story and your story. One person is the world entire.

Asking the same question, over and over again, of a collection of people living in a closed setting, now so fortunate as to obtain health care, nutritional care and education in a city like Doha, was not easy. At one point, it occurred to me that the place bringing them together was the true face of the world, and that we – people walking on two feet – were the exception. As the days passed, it only became harder. Every day, I went to the government office in Thumama next to Hamad International Airport and I would tell myself that tomorrow would be easier, but each day was more difficult than the last. These survivors, whose stories I wanted to be a means of reconstructing the world that was destroyed, had lost everything: their families, their homes, their land, their limbs. I wondered to myself: should they have to relate their experiences of the war? Contrary to my expectations, however, it was they who wanted to tell their stories, and they were determined that the world should hear them, despite their despair at what had happened. They were generous and cheerful, brimming with ideas and beliefs about the meaning of life, and they still believed in the possibility of understanding something of this reality. Most of them wanted to return to Gaza after their treatment was finished. All, without exception, were unarmed civilians, ordinary people. Most were from the new generation who knew nothing beyond Gaza's borders.

At first, I thought this book of testimonies would focus solely on women, but with time, and after seeing the numbers of children and teenagers, I decided to meet with as many people as possible and to make a selection. Most testimonies were filled with silence, that conspicuous, deadly silence which can only be expressed through corresponding silence. At a certain point, I reflected that a book about the memory of loss and erasure meant, in short, a book with blank pages, because in most cases silence was more eloquent than words. They tried to find words and were generous in sharing their feelings – I was their perpetual guest.

We have a tendency to sanctify the agony of victims, but in one way or another they made me feel that they needed no sympathy. The people of Gaza don't need our pity, but our acknowledgement of their bravery, their dignity and their rights, and their urgent wish to disclose the truth of their tragedy.

They had many questions, and their meanings altered, and post-disaster fears appeared, and of course there was post-traumatic stress. Some of them spent days talking about the people they had lost, and who they had been and the beauty of their city, Gaza, the city which deep down they realized no longer existed. Their ages ranged from 13 to 65, they were men, women and children, and they came from a variety of social backgrounds. The majority were educated, including women had mainly married young and who were now mothers, grandmothers and aunts accompanying members of their families.

I didn't get into direct political questions with them; instead, the focus was on their lives and how they had survived the genocide, or whatever facts of their tragedies they were able to relate. But this was sufficient for my need to document and to restore future-oriented memories. Most had witnessed the largest massacres, such as those at the Indonesian Hospital and al-Shifa Hospital. The doctor I met was one of the medical personnel at al-Shifa Hospital and he personally witnessed the actions of the Israeli army towards the patients and their carers. I also met patients who experienced that same event. The repetition found in the testimonies, the multitude of questions, formed a wider picture of the imagination-defying savagery of the genocide, the gross desecrations of human rights that the Israeli army commits with respect to women, children and the elderly. This necessitated a recurrence of some events in the selected testimonies; I found them to be confirmation of the methodical approach characteristic of genocide, although I have removed many of the more horrifying details.

These people were not discussing the conduct of Hamas, or the resistance, or even the fate of Palestine.* They

* Translator's note: There are several armed factions within Gaza, including Hamas and its armed wing, which are in conflict with Israel. These various groups have different names and political agendas, but are referred to under the umbrella term 'the resistance' within testimonies. In general, the witnesses distinguish between Hamas and the wider resistance movement, but some appear to conflate them. [Unless otherwise indicated, every note is a translator's note.]

were speaking about themselves as people, as peaceful civilians. They spoke about their torn and broken bodies. They made their disclosures sincerely and spontaneously, and they wanted the world to hear their stories. In their narratives, the witnesses were unanimous that the Israelis were not solely acting in retaliation for the attacks of Hamas. They repeated the expression I have heard many times in the last few months: 'We have lived through war for decades, and now we are living through genocide.'

The children and young people were the most silent, and their testimonies appear short in comparison with the others. They were the keenest to speak and the most insistent on telling their stories, but silence cheated them. Their sentences were brief and struggled to come out, as if they were unable to find the right words. There was a teenager called Abdullah, 13 years old, who had an effect on me that I have never experienced since I began documenting atrocities in 2011. He was different; he spoke without stopping, and he asked many questions. This child, whose family burned to death in front of him in a UNRWA bus, told me he wasn't a child, insisting that there were no children in Gaza. A condition of childhood, as he said, is that they live among their books, their schools and their families, and all this was permanently out of reach in Gaza. He didn't laugh and he moved slowly. He behaved like a man, speaking and moving like he was 30 years old, but his burned face and the gleam in his eyes reminded me that he was still a child. He showed me pictures of himself before he was injured, insisting that I see a photo of his family. Several others did exactly the same; they all wanted me to see a photo of their families before they vanished from existence. Most had lost family members, but spoke about them and addressed them as if they were still there.

For me, the most terrifying thing was a novel detail. I had not come across it when documenting the revolution and the war in Syria, nor had I heard of it in other wars, however brutal they were. This was a sophisticated method and instrument of murder, for although the barrel bombs that fell on the Gazans had been used in Syria, and although fire belts – a rain of missiles falling without pause on the same area for up to an hour, which destroys entire tower blocks – are not used in other places, they can be imagined. What cannot be imagined, however, is the unleashing of algorithms of murder, the use of artificial intelligence to kill. This perpetual human terror – of letting a machine do to a human exactly what it was built for – has been made reality in Gaza. The Israeli government has taken humanity as a whole to the threshold of this horror. They have killed using AI programmes, according to Human Rights Watch . Murder no longer requires a human decision; there is no longer a moment of human hesitation before pulling the trigger. AI algorithms, built upon millions of data of death and destruction, understand perfectly when and where and how to murder Gazans. Man, with all his attendant fears and conflicting feelings, has become a gap to be closed, merely an onlooker to a crime conducted by his digital shadow.

The most dangerous part is that this level of brutality seeks not only to kill, but to subjugate. AI does not only fight bodies, but minds. It seeks to control feelings, to broadcast fear and terror into people's souls. Murder is no longer the only aim – total subjection is.

War is no longer war as we know it. It is an exercise controlled by posthuman software, where aims are separated from means and the physical capacity for combat.

Algorithms decide who should live and who should die. There is no place here for the human concept of hostility; Palestinians have become merely undesirable data.

Wars conducted through AI are nothing but simulations – but lethal simulations. According to the logic of Jean Baudrillard's simulations, murder here is 'second-stage' murder, where the act is separated from its physical reality. Drones bomb cities, people, women, children, on the orders of algorithms, while human soldiers sit in insulated control rooms, drinking tea and laughing as they observe real destruction through screens, devoid of blood or screams. Life is turned into mere code, and death into a human state digitally translated.

Unmanned aerial vehicles, which Gazans are unsure what to call, appear in their accounts with the name 'zannana' (or 'zannanat' in plural), the Palestinian expression for 'drone'. But in this war there was a new name, a new horror, a 'flying killing machine', as people called it: a quadcopter. The witness accounts are cut through with the horror of these deadly, mythical beings. They enter houses, bedrooms, stop over children's heads, issue instructions, shoot in the head, take iris scans, shoot in the eye, accompany the lines of those who are displaced and escaping bombardment and forced to leave their homes, remaining above their heads to compel them to flee. These are scenes we can only conceive of as something from a science fiction film, but now they have become reality. During the siege of the Indonesian Hospital, there was a woman who couldn't look at the window because these killer drones were hovering there, outside the window; any movement guaranteed a bullet, an automated response from this killer drone. This advanced machinery displayed the kind of skill and precision in the act of murder that made Gazan hearts bleed, making their life under bombardment and siege a double hell.

When it came to the personal lives of the women, the abuses that happened to them, there was total reserve. None of the women, part of Gaza's conservative society, wanted to dive into her intimate suffering. There was intense shame for what was done to them, and I believe that social surveillance played a significant role, along with the stigma and shame they felt in speaking about their bodies and their privacy. One woman related how she suffered from vaginal bleeding as a result of being exposed to poisoned bombs. Nour, a journalist, related female suffering of another kind, about the lack of sanitary towels and the challenges of having a period, about deprivation of the barest minimum of hygiene, about the lack of babies' nappies. Women would tell me about rape and harassment that had happened to other women, but I did not include these incidents in the testimonies because I did not hear from those it happened to. When it came to their own experiences, the women would deny having been personally subject to any such abuse.

Only one witness told me her atrocious suffering as a woman in a society that treated women as second-class persons. She asked that I call her by the letter S and remove anything that might indicate her identity, even though what she related was not a sexual violation. Rather, it was a profound moment of sadness and revelation returning her to her former life, a moment of aggregate violence as she lay under the rubble on the verge of death; this is where the most brutal forms of cruelty are made manifest, between straightforward murder and genocide, and the other, moral, murder of women. S related how she was changed and decided to rebel against her society. Isra, too, spoke of a different facet of the war. Her life changed and she began to tend to others, volunteering as a nurse.

It is not true that women are only victims; in fact, these women worked side by side alongside men, rescuing the wounded, working in medicine and nursing, as in Huda's case. These are stories about the compassionate human spirit, about the loftiness of the human soul in the midst of war, as if we are seeing a scene from myth made flesh. Despite the hideousness of war, I saw human beauty in the lives of these women.

The choice of which testimonies to include in the book was extremely challenging. There is one testimony of an entire family, told from the point of view of the mother and father – theirs is unique in this context. The accounts do not adhere to a single formula or a fixed number of words, especially when describing conditions in the hospitals, displacement, checkpoints, the carefully considered method of bombardment. In the same way, the language used generally belonged to the witness and thus varies in its style and mode of expression. I preferred to leave each testimony as it was without trying to unify the narrative, especially where the women desired to speak at greater length and in painful detail. So I followed the manner of each person, leaving their expressions and the level of their language untouched, removing some phrases that were directed at me personally but leaving in others if I felt, in that moment, that I represented the entire world they wanted to address. Equally, I left some words in the local Gazan dialect, such as 'sidi' when referring to a grandfather, and 'dar' instead of family name. I tried not to include too many accounts in which the same reactions and experiences recurred, in order to form a broader picture of the agonies of these people who accord life great value, and cling to it until their last breath.

The testimonies did not depend on a single approach – some are long, others are short. The short testimonies contained considerable silence, and as silence is a language in itself, I left it in. As for the long testimonies, the witnesses wanted to speak, but some I was forced to shorten. Overall, I find that such variety represents an attempt to encompass the various modes of expression and thought, an attempt to articulate tragedy and pain, to reflect on language and narrate disaster.

Out of all the testimonies I recorded and the speakers whose lives I followed, I have included just two testimonies from young men living in Gaza, and who are still there, inside the Strip.* I recorded dozens of such testimonies through the internet, but despite their power and their importance, I preferred not to use them. This is because, for me, an important factor in the legitimacy of this book lay in my personal relationship with those I spoke to, my presence alongside them and my participation in their daily lives. Nevertheless, I retain my faith in the need to write about the besieged who are still, even now, facing bombardment, murder, displacement and starvation. Perhaps that will form a future project.

In closing, I place these testimonies, the others I have recorded in my books and those which I will record in the future into history's safekeeping, to remain as a testament to the human hope for salvation from oppression; testament to a dream of justice for those living beneath the grindstone of this violent era. It is our duty as writers, activists and intellectuals, the very least we can do, to challenge the act of destruction: we must rebuild the world with words, so that perhaps one day, the justice that has been so ardently pursued can finally be realized.

Samar Yazbek
September 2024, Paris

* These are the testimonies of Muhannad Radwan and Muhammad Fadi Saleh.

—

More than a year has passed since I finished this book, and although the world is discussing the ceasefire, it is far from being a reality while Israel is still bombing hospitals and their surroundings, even now. This has not been discussed much in the media. In point of fact the ceasefire has been violated several times by Israel, and Gazan victims number in the hundreds. The truth is there is no ceasefire to speak of.

Perhaps I can say that, in the time since compiling this book of testimonies, famine has been wielded as a weapon, claiming a large number of victims. The massacre did not stop with the events testified to in these pages; rather, they were followed by a new art form of murder. Along with murder by artificial intelligence, Israel has instigated the weapon of starvation against the people of Gaza.

According to a statement issued by the Ministry of Health in Gaza on 1 October 2025, the confirmed number of deaths in the Strip through starvation and malnutrition has risen to 455, including 151 children.* I did not record this new method of genocide against the Gazans in the testimonies; when the process of starving Gazans and using famine as a weapon of war began, I said to myself that perhaps it was a reverberation from other wars around the globe. But after following what is happening on the ground in Gaza daily and attentively, I have found that Israel used starvation and death from starvation as another form of systematic genocide. The pictures arriving in succession through the media and news agencies were appalling, and I would wonder to myself to what

* See Sana Noor Haq, Rachel Wilson, Soph Warnes, Lou Robinson and Henrik Pettersson, 'How Israeli actions caused famine in Gaza, visualized', CNN, 2 October 2025.

depths the moral shame of the human race will descend, when we stand thus, arms crossed, in front of children who are dying from hunger. Their figures were like moving skeletons, slowly dying every day in front of our eyes and the eyes of the entire world.

On 23 October 2025, the World Health Organization announced that 'the situation in Gaza still remains catastrophic because what's entering [Gaza] is not enough'.* The organization has not recorded any improvement in hunger levels among Gazans, confirming that the nutritional and health situation has not changed despite the ceasefire, which of course has subsequently been violated by Israel.

The painful truth that persists in the details and grief of the people of Gaza is that forms of brutality have been diversifying and increasing, and the horrifying testimonies I gathered were only the beginning of a systematic process of murder. I was struck by something like numb shock when I realized that even the mechanism of destroying the hospitals was systematic. The wounded were murdered slowly, in the sense that the hospitals continued to be targeted with the aim of killing the greatest possible number of survivors, and after the ceasefire, hospitals such as al-Shifa were re-targeted. We are confronted with the word 'survivor' taking on new and paradoxical dimensions: whoever survived a bomb or missile cannot really be called a 'survivor' because they remain in imminent danger. Wounded patients in the hospitals become perpetual targets of the Israeli killing machine.

In truth, after all this time, I was hopeful that there

* Tedros Adhanom Ghebreyesus, chief of the World Health Organization, quoted in Abby Rogers, AFP and Reuters, 'Hunger crisis in Gaza is "catastrophic" despite ceasefire, WHO chief says', *Al Jazeera*, 23 October 2024.

would be a reduction in the killing and suffering of Gazans, a building of bridges of peace in the region, but another year has passed and still we are falling into the abyss. Perhaps there is a more important question for me as I continue my project of constructing humanity's collective memory, and which relies on the theory that 'the personal is political': Was I right to record these testimonies?

Perhaps, to my crushing disappointment, for all these lives I collected, believing I would defend victims who resisted death and lost pieces of their bodies and lives – perhaps I have done nothing but add a black stain to human history. A stain of words... the words of the people of Gaza.

November 2025, Paris

NASMA AL-FARRA (UM YAHYA)
31 years old
Khan Younis

On that Saturday in October, I was preparing breakfast
for my children when we heard the sound of bombs.
Yahya, my 11-year-old son, was getting ready to go to
school, but after hearing the bombs he stayed at home, we
wouldn't let him go. From the sound of the rockets and
from the news going around the street, we understood
that the resistance had attacked Israel in an unprecedented manner. I was very frightened, and I realized that this
time wouldn't be like the previous wars.

We were expecting to be bombed, we were actually
waiting for it. That's what stopped me from sleeping until
dawn over the following nights – I was frightened they
would bomb us while we were asleep. I would stare at the
ceiling all night, not knowing when it was going to fall on
us. On the morning of 10 October, my husband – Abu
Yahya* – asked me what food we needed. Yahya asked to
go with his father, but my husband said no. We were terrified to let our children go outside in the street because we
were expecting to be bombed.

I have five children: Yahya, Sara, Sama, Lama and
Leen. Yahya is the only boy. Little Leen, 8 years old, said,
'Mama, I'm hungry,' and asked me for a sandwich. I got
up to go with her to the kitchen, Yahya followed and
asked for my phone, then he headed to the living room. In
those few seconds, our life changed forever.

At first, my brain couldn't interpret what had

---

* Abu Yahya is a kunya, a respectful title whereby a parent is
  referred to using the name of their eldest child or eldest son. In
  this instance, Nasma al-Farra is called Um Yahya (Yahya's mother).
  The testimony that follows is given by Abu Yahya (Yahya's father).

happened. All of a sudden, I found myself covered in black dust and smoke – I didn't even hear the bomb. I screamed and shouted my children's names, I could hear my voice, but it was as though it wasn't me shouting, like it was someone else looking for their children. I couldn't see anything because of the smoke. Leen... I screamed Leen's name, I found her next to me and picked her up and tried to get out, but fire scorched my face. I went back to the kitchen, the missile was still burning there, a terrible fire. The fire went out. I ran and ran, there was wreckage all around me. The house was completely destroyed, I couldn't see anything. I wanted to get Leen out of the rubble and look for her brother and sisters. I found that the stairs had been destroyed, I couldn't go down to take my daughter outside. We were living on the second floor, the destruction surrounded us. Our whole neighbourhood had been levelled. I called for my children, I was stuck on the second floor with my daughter, and I could see people's body parts scattered all around.

A young man came and took Leen off me and got her downstairs – a few young men had gathered around the rubble. I refused to come down without my other children, Sara, Lama, Sama and Yahya. I found Sara. Her face was completely burned and so were her hands. She was walking right in front of me, full of burns, she was walking back and forth. I shouted. I was screaming and I didn't know whether my voice was coming from my throat: 'Sara! Sara! Come here! Where is your sister? Where is Sama? Come over here!' Her body was burned, but she could walk. She was walking and in a lot of pain, she was walking and refusing help. She looked around, stunned, and walked forwards. She crawled down the stairs. She was right there in front of me, in silent agony, crawling over the rubble, refusing any help. I screamed and screamed, 'Sama! Yahya!' I heard Lama's voice, she was under the rubble, under the wall. I knelt down and tried to lift it with my hands, but I couldn't. I clawed at it with my fingers, perhaps it would crumble.

My husband appeared, and like me he screamed the children's names. Then he was carrying Sama in his arms. I didn't understand. My daughters, my twin girls, 15 years old, were right there, one walking in silence with burns, the other a lifeless corpse in her father's arms. My husband took Sama downstairs, they asked me to come too but I refused. The young men who had come to help were digging, pulling the children from the first floor out from under the rubble. My husband returned with his father and they began to dig. They found Yahya, they brought out Lama. Yahya died of internal bleeding a few hours later in Nasser Hospital in Khan Younis, and Lama's leg was amputated the following day.

They took my daughter Lama to intensive care, her head was split open to the middle of her forehead. She needed three stitches from the top of her eye to the middle of her forehead. There was a large wound on her hand. And she needed a lot of blood. The doctor tried to save her injured leg, she stayed in surgery for hours. During that time they buried Sama, they buried her at six o'clock in the morning, then they buried Yahya. They made me watch the video. I couldn't move from the hospital. My son Yahya was buried after my daughter Sama. Two of my children were buried and I wasn't there. Nine martyrs from my husband's family, they couldn't take their bodies out whole. They were torn to pieces – they buried them in plastic bags. My brother, the doctor, said, 'If Lama's leg isn't amputated, she will die. Do you want your daughter to die?' The next day, Lama's leg was amputated. She would have been poisoned if they hadn't done it. I asked,

'Where is my daughter's leg?' They said, 'We buried it.' They buried it just anywhere! They buried it with all the other amputated limbs. My sister's husband came and took her leg out of that place and buried it next to the graves of Yahya and Sama, so at least it could remain with her brother and sister. Sara, my burned daughter, was completely silent and refused to speak. She didn't want to hear about her twin sister buried with her brother. It seemed as though we had entered hell. During that time I was in Nasser Hospital with my husband, I was in the burns ward with Sara, and my other daughter Lama was in intensive care, her face was torn open and her leg was amputated. We stayed in the hospital for twenty-five days. They let us stay because our house was destroyed. We were in the hospital with our two wounded daughters. The bombing beside Nasser Hospital went on continuously for two consecutive nights. Sometimes, we were forced to carry the patients out of the hospital in their beds, with missiles raining down on us from every direction, and glass landing everywhere. The corridor was full of displaced people. The hospital held displaced people, doctors, patients and their families, all these people were squashed into the narrow corridor. There were a large number of children who had been burned by phosphorus. Two girls with us, Layal and Abla Zannoun, had faces burned by phosphorus. I still remember how my daughter climbed over the stairs in the middle of the rubble, how she crawled, how she couldn't cry. How she screamed when they changed her dressings, her screams are still in my ears. She wouldn't let them change her dressings unless I was there. I wasn't able to look at her wounds, I couldn't bear it. She still wants only her mother. My daughter flung on the ground screaming, that image of her is still in my head.

32

SAMIR AL-AGHA (ABU YAHYA)
54 years old
Khan Younis

My son Yahya was 11 years old when he left me. The Israelis killed him. He used to play football in a sports club, they won a championship the day before the war. We in Gaza have been under siege since 2000, ever since the second Intifada. When we went to university there were checkpoints, they would close the roads for no reason, we weren't able to go to university every day. This was happening in Gaza before Hamas' rule, from the days of Abu Ammar.* We have lived under siege for a quarter of a century, and the siege got worse in the Hamas era. Gaza has been a large prison since then.

The first war on Gaza in the Hamas era was in 2008. It began while children were going to school, at nine o'clock in the morning. The Israelis targeted military sites at first, they killed a lot of Hamas fighters, then they set about killing civilians. In the 2012 war, the Israelis began to send messages demanding that we evacuate our houses as a preliminary to bombing them. They would bomb after a few minutes, or a few hours, or a few days. Sometimes they didn't bomb at all, and at other times they destroyed houses over the heads of the people inside without any warning. They waged a psychological war. People began to stop leaving their homes – let them kill us here! Where would we go? Our neighbour, from Dar al-Astal,† stayed in his house and wouldn't leave, as if he was saying to them, 'Just kill us and be done with it.'

Yahya was born in 2013. The Israelis had assassinated

---

* Abu Ammar is the kunya of Yasser Arafat (1929–2004), the Palestinian political leader.

† Dar al-Astal – the al-Astal family.

one of the Hamas leadership – Ahmed al-Jabari – in Sheikh Radwan, then there was a war. That war went on for fifty-one days, it was during Ramadan. Violent artillery fire targeted us. We went about our lives displaced, constantly worried for our families and children. We bought things from the market, afraid. We were afraid to get in the car, we were afraid to get out of it, we were afraid to walk, we were afraid to stop. Our lives were continuous fear. We went out a little in the short periods of calm between wars. That was how we grew up, how we married, how we had our children, and how our children died. The death didn't only just begin – we have been dying for a long time.

The wars carried on after that, but they never measured up to what's happening now. This is genocide, not war.

I want my son to grow up, to be a doctor or an engineer, to have children of his own. We want all our children to grow up, but they die before our very eyes. For over seventy years, everyone has abandoned us.

At twenty past six in the morning on 7 October, Yahya was on his way to his exam, but he came home because he had forgotten his water bottle and before I knew it the world had exploded all around us. The rockets came out of Gaza. We were afraid and stayed home, we didn't know what was happening, then we learned from the news that Hamas had attacked. We saw the resistance in the streets, we saw them capturing hostages. I realized that terrible punishments were in store for us, so we began to pack our bags. We believed that war would break out between two sides, we never thought they would carry out this attack and then we would be left to die.

We had our bags packed and by the door in readiness for us to displace to the middle of Gaza, we took all our identity documents. The electricity was cut off. I asked my wife, 'What food do you want to make?' We were carrying on as if we were going to live forever, but we knew we might die at any moment. She would have made kousa mahshy for the children, but they never ate it.

Yahya and his sister wanted to come to the market with me, but I was afraid they would bomb us on the way. Before I had gone very far, I heard it. I turned around and there was a grey cloud covering our building. It covered most of the street. Debris was flying all around me. It was a barrel bomb the Israeli army had dropped. In our area, there were no fighters. I was nailed to the spot, I couldn't move. I looked around, trying to move, but I couldn't. I saw them, my brother and his family and his children, being brought out from under the rubble.

Finally, I ran and got inside the building. There was wreckage everywhere. I tried to crawl and look around, there was nothing but dust and piles of rubble. I fell over and crashed into the wall, then the rubble collapsed and I fell with it, and finally I was able to go up to our home. I found Um Yahya there, holding onto Leen. She was all white, completely covered with dust from the wreckage. The dust from the missile was black, the black stayed under Um Yahya's nails for two months, however much she tried to scrub it away. My daughter's wounds, too – the bomb split her face open – the wounds stayed black. The black dust from the bomb and the missile coloured the wounds.

When I saw Um Yahya, I asked, 'Where are the children?' I was looking all around and saw that the house had vanished and the walls were gone, it was just a hill of rubble. I couldn't see my children, I didn't see Yahya.

I looked around. I didn't recognize the house. I was standing in empty space next to my house, and I couldn't find it at all. Something inside me disappeared, I couldn't find myself. I saw my wife, then I saw my daughter Sara – she was burned, walking and crawling in silence. One of them came and took Sara. I kept looking everywhere for the children like a madman, searching under the rubble and debris, but I couldn't find them. I saw how stone fell from the window. I saw, under the debris, through a gap in the middle of the rubble, I saw my daughter Sama. There she was, lying on her bed. I pulled her out and looked into her face. I knew she had departed this life. I began screaming and shouting for someone to come and help me. I was very weak, I couldn't speak. I was looking at her face. I stared at her injuries for a long time. Her head was split open, her features were difficult to make out. She was such a beautiful girl, so delicate. I asked them to cover her up. I looked at her and screamed, 'Ya Allah... Ya Allah.' And I also shouted, 'Where are the rest of my children?' I recognized her by the braces on her teeth, that was how I used to tell her apart from her twin. Afterwards, I learned that her braces was the distinguishing mark recorded by her name in the morgue.*

After they took Sama, I started looking for Lama and Yahya. I heard sounds and voices, and at last I saw Lama. She was under the rubble, screaming. I was relieved she was still alive. Her leg was hanging strangely and her head was split open. I gave her to the young men who were next to me, and I carried on searching until I heard Yahya's groans. I found him and I brought him out from under the rubble. The doctors didn't notice the bleeding in his liver. They put him in intensive care with Lama, in Nasser Hospital in Khan Younis. I didn't know my

* Due to the difficulties of identifying heavily disfigured corpses, it has become common practice in Gaza to include a distinguishing feature when recording a death, by which the body might be recognized.

children's fate when we pulled them out. I only knew that Sama had died.

My uncle's house, a three-storey building, was reduced to piles of rubble within minutes. Nine people died in that building from my uncle's family. All of them. An entire family vanished, from grandfather to grandchildren. In seconds, I lived between two lives. I was in one life, and all of a sudden I was in another life. We are human and we want to live, we have children and we want them to live. The people of Gaza have an obsession for educating their children, we exhaust ourselves and we wear ourselves to the bone so our children will be educated. My daughter Sama was like the breeze, refined and quiet and hard-working, different from the other girls of her generation. When she started growing up, I could see the extent of her insight and intelligence, she was one of the outstanding students in her class. She had the most beautiful fingers in the world.

The world collapsed around us. Buildings were destroyed, people vanished and flesh was kneaded with fire and stone and metal. We are burned up here, from the inside.

Our lives revolved around our children. All my life was for them, those children of ours, and we wanted them to live. We have died alongside them.

After the house was bombed and we went to the hospital, I saw everyone around me calling out Lama's name. They thought I didn't know about Sama's death. I was asking about Lama, frightened she had died as well. There was such chaos and terror. I went to the morgue, corpses upon corpses, and the people around me, those people were trying to identify their children, the bodies were disfigured, everyone was looking for whatever was left of their children. People were condoling with each other, everyone had their dead.

We buried Sama. Yahya and Lama were still in intensive care, and my third daughter Sara had severe burns on her face. We left the funeral, and I left Sama under the soil. The following day, my son Yahya died. I couldn't believe it. I hadn't expected him to go like that. I didn't find any wounds on his body, he seemed fine. They had discovered the bleed too late. In the middle of the night, they took Yahya to the morgue. I was thinking of his mother, how she was going to find out and how she would take the news. When I told her, she was silent. She didn't even yell. She said, 'Alhamdulillah wa hasbi Allah wa ni'm al-wakil' * and then she cried in silence. She cried a lot in silence. We went to a second funeral. I was crying.

Our relatives took my daughter's leg and buried it in the graveyard. They did it out of care for me, they were trying to spare me this situation, but the leg was buried at random between the graves of two people we don't know. To my relatives it was just a girl's leg, but it was part of my daughter, part of my beloved daughter who is still alive. It's odd that parts of people are buried while they are still alive. We brought my daughter's leg and buried it next to her brother and sister. Family has to stay together.

* Alhamdulillah means 'Thanks be to God'.
  The second prayer, 'Hasbi Allah wa ni'm al-wakil', derives from
  Qur'an 3:173 and can be loosely translated as 'I trust in Him'.
  The practice of thanking God after a tragedy is a way of showing
  faith in God's divine plan.

KHALED ABU SAMRA
30 years old
Al-Shifa Hospital

On Saturday 7 October, I was supposed to finish my night shift at the hospital at seven in the morning. Exactly twenty minutes before that, at precisely twenty minutes to seven in the morning, the baying of savage rockets joined the waves on the sea, fracturing the morning silence of Gaza. We stopped in our tracks, stunned. We didn't realize at first where the sound came from, or why, or who it was that began the bombing. Our bewilderment didn't last long, and we soon discovered that the missiles had been launched from our side, from the land we stood upon, the Gaza Strip. We believed, initially, that leadership figures like Salih al-Aroury or Ziyad Nakhala had been assassinated, and these rockets were a response of the kind Gaza had grown familiar with in recent years. We calmly readied the emergency equipment, as if it was just another training drill. Dr Jamal al-Harazin, Dr Muataz Harara and I, we knew that vengeance would be very great, but our minds were incapable of imagining, or perhaps we refused to imagine, the volume of blood that the Israelis would spill this time. I haven't left the hospital since then.

Injuries began flooding in. Vehicles, whether ambulances or private cars, arrived, deposited their human cargo, then went away to save more. Moments of delay were calculated in blood and martyrs, and wounded people, carried on people's shoulders, kept coming. Doctors in Gaza are well aware they are fated to come face to face with a massacre, but this time lethal injuries were coming from every corner of the Strip. There seemed to be massacres in more than one place; wounded and martyrs

39

from a bombing on a popular market in the north of the Strip, wounded and dead in a bombing on a school in the centre of Gaza City. By that afternoon, we had lost count of the number of massacres. As for the martyrs, we were counting them in tens: ten here, twenty there, twenty-something across here and here. The gates of hell were opened onto Gaza. What I saw was like the horrors of Judgement Day.

The sound of Israeli bombardment began reaching the whole area of the Gaza Strip. Did I say area? The territory of Gaza is too small to be considered even as much as that. I was completely overwhelmed. My family were in Tel Zaatar in Jabalia Camp, to the north. I heard that the bombing there was very heavy, so I tried to get some news of them. I was also thinking of my fiancée. I remained torn between the wounded people and the body parts in my hands, and my family and fiancée. The bombing carried death everywhere, hell everywhere.

They were bombing incessantly. From the outset, we realized clearly that they wanted total annihilation of all residents of the Strip. Any living being on the territory of Gaza is considered a target for bombing and destruction. From the first day, they breached all limits and all human rights laws. We said goodbye to our first responder colleague Tariq in the first hours. Tariq Ashour, he was one of the best of men, the most encouraging and kind. He fell to bombardment on the first day, while he was tending to the wounded. They killed him while he was carrying out his work.

The Baptist Hospital is no more than five kilometres from al-Shifa. I was there when body parts started arriving, limbs of the displaced people who had been inside the hospital when it was bombed. Most came as charred corpses.

That day, the director of the hospital, Dr Muhammad Abu Salmiya, asked everyone in the medical teams to go down to the emergency ward immediately. The ward was full of human limbs, blackened corpses and people looking for their relatives. It was like being in one of the chambers of hell. The beds were full, there were bodies on the floor, there were wounded people and blood in the corridors between the wards, mothers were weeping, the living were holding the hands of the featureless dead and refusing to leave them, a boy was blowing air into a dismembered woman's corpse, trying to bring her back to life – she was his mother. Another man was collecting pieces of a child's body. A thread of black and red blood collected to form a small stream that one of them wiped off the tiles.

They brought in a severely burned 15-year-old girl who was screaming, and next to her was the blackened body of another girl. They were sisters from the al-Kahlout family. I started to treat the first girl, trying to reassure her. She was shouting, 'There's nothing wrong with me, there's nothing wrong with me, where is my sister? Her name is Amani Kahlout.' She was crying and shouting her sister's name, looking for her. The dead girl next to her was her sister, so charred that she hadn't recognized her.

We took the girl out of the emergency ward and put her sister with the martyrs. I completely collapsed at that moment and considered walking out. I was incapable of speech. I tried to pull myself together once again, thinking of my duty, the duty I owed these victims. I did, and I carried on. The hardest times came in the evening, when changing my surgical gown. I would collapse as I looked at my bloodstained clothes. In those moments, I would start crying, alone in my room. Death was my daily life, with bodies that were torn and burned, dead children, and at the end of every day my clothes were smeared with blood. What was the most painful of all? The mothers. They were what hurt the most, the mothers surrounding me all the time, asking about the fate of their children. They believed I could save their children. How many times would I reply, and in how many ways, that their children had died?

The al-Shifa complex is constituted by three primary buildings: the emergency building, the specialty building and the maternity building, along with the branch buildings for administration and warehousing. The complex, the biggest in all of the Gaza Strip, offers medical services to over a million Gazans. So when Israel began its ground offensive at the beginning of November, and they distributed leaflets ordering people to head south of Wadi Gaza, we knew they intended to storm the complex. The plan to force people out was clear, and implementing it required depriving people of first response services, and then of the remaining medical services.

At first, they began bombing the hospital surroundings. It was a psychological war to compel more than 70,000 displaced people and patients to leave the complex. As the bombardment of Gaza City intensified, most of the hospital buildings became a first response service. I specialize in cardiology, and I kept working in the cardiology department along with my additional work in the emergency department. The Israeli machinery of murder worked around the clock; massacres occurred around the clock; the wounded arrived at the hospital around the clock. The al-Shifa complex was more or less the only defence barrier for anyone fortunate enough to survive the successive daily massacres across all northern Gaza. The bombing spread from the environs of the complex to include both the maternity ward and the laundry, followed by the administrative offices, and then they targeted the intensive care building. We called all the media outlets we could reach, we were shouting to the whole world that the Israeli army was attacking the al-Shifa complex with its 70,000 patients and displaced people, but the world left us alone. Our calls for help were futile.

The Israeli tanks encircled us. They prevented new wounded patients from reaching the hospital; the patients and displaced people inside the complex, including us, were prisoners without electricity, water or food. We were surrounded by snipers, tanks and zannanat.* There were a number of critical cases who weren't able to leave – discharging them in their state meant killing them, so there was no choice but to remain steadfast.† We collected water and tinned food in the emergency department, and prepared ourselves for a siege whose duration we had no way of knowing. The engineer responsible for the electrical supplies was able to maintain a current, restricted to the emergency ward for those kept alive by artificial breathing apparatus, and to incubators for premature babies. We had some fuel stored before the siege and we brought in additional fuel donated by some of Gaza's private petrol stations. This small reserve wouldn't suffice

---

* Author's note: Zannana (pl: zannanat). This Palestinian expression for drone will be repeated many times in the testimonies. Gazans are familiar with a lethal type of these drones called a quadcopter – a flying machine with four propellers. These machines form a particular horror to the people of Gaza because they carry out tasks of shooting, taking photographs and giving orders. They also have the distinction of recognizing faces. In the testimonies, the witnesses will use all these terms – drone, zannana and quadcopter.

† The Arabic word Khaled uses is sumud.
This is a term closely associated with various stages of Palestinian non-violent resistance since the 1967 war with Israel.

for much, but by restricting our use of electricity to that equipment, it would give those ravaged bodies a little more time to keep clinging on to their souls.

Death was a mercy, I would tell myself, every time we lifted the breathing equipment off someone who had surrendered their soul. I had read about doctors in other wars who gave their patients an ampule of merciful death. Every time I looked into the eyes of the doctors in the hospital, I felt as though we had all sworn to cling onto our patients' souls, to their last breath.

Everything inside the hospital building was reliant on us. At first it seemed strange – doctors and nurses and carers and technicians, all of us doing the cleaning, preparing food, acting as psychologists. And then we became journalists – they cut off the phone network across all of al-Shifa to cut off news of us to the world, for three days. We had to do something. I knew there was weak coverage in the bridge that linked two buildings in the complex. I would go there to check on my family, but there was a problem – the area was exposed and anyone who went there was an easy target for snipers. We used to crawl, avoiding the snipers' lenses and their drones. We did this more than fifty times, we had to communicate this information to the outside world. At night the snipers would send laser beams sweeping across the whole area and we crawled throughout it all. Now, I can't believe how we did it. Everyone was ready to die, just to share news of the patients with the outside world. The water and food began to run out, our lips were blanched and cracked with thirst, so that it became difficult at first sight to distinguish the patient from the doctor.

The children began to collapse under the weight of hunger. They were so emaciated, the scythe of death seemed to be hovering over them. One of the paramedics' wives learned from her husband there might be some tinned food in a room at the entrance to the hospital, and she decided to confront the Israeli army. This woman went outside, followed by three others, and headed towards that room surrounded by tanks. That defied belief, four women facing off alone against a battalion of soldiers bristling with snipers and encased in armour. Behind the doors, we were calling for them to come back, but they kept going. Red lasers from the Israeli snipers' rifles began to make their way towards the women's bodies and heads. We were screaming at them to come back but they weren't afraid and they ignored us. I almost lost my mind. I already knew that a single second separated the laser beam and the bullet. After that I don't know what happened or how it happened, but I realized my feet were sprinting my body towards the women. I hurled myself in front of them and began shouting short phrases that I knew in Hebrew, 'I'm a doctor, don't shoot, I'm a doctor.' Red beams began to slide slowly over my face. My life flashed before my eyes in that moment. I was prepared to die, perhaps even seeking it out, demanding it.

Come here by yourself, came an Israeli soldier's voice in Arabic through a loudspeaker. *Take off your clothes and raise your hands.* I carried out their orders with the discipline of a hostage. I remained naked, my hands in the air, and I started to yell and vow that there was no one inside apart from patients. I kept on screaming, 'We have lost all the necessities of life, food and water, everyone will soon die of hunger and thirst. I swear, there is no one here apart from patients, women and children with serious injuries, and wounded civilians.' I looked down at myself; I was still naked. Then I repeated the same words, without stopping, I was only asking for food and water. I directed my speech at the whole company of soldiers, 'Most of them are children, come and see for yourself, come in, they are just kids crying from hunger.'

It was my first time meeting the Israeli army face to face. I live in Gaza which they have turned into a large prison, they have besieged us and prevented us from entering and leaving for years, they have killed us with their missiles for years, and this was my first time meeting them in person. Later that night, they said to us: *Come here, we've brought you some water!* We believed them. They allowed us to move from one building to another so we could bring the water they said they had brought. But this was a lie. They hadn't brought us any water. They simply allowed us to move to another building where we had been storing water before the siege. They had stripped the Arabic stickers off the cases of water, and put stickers written in Hebrew on top of them that said: *Presented by the Israeli Defence Force*. I understood that they took pictures and distributed them to the media, so they could claim they'd brought us water. I thought I was going to explode. They were killing us, then lying.

We had nothing left apart from a few dates, so we fed them to the wounded. We drank brine out of tins. I gave my wounded brother some dates. They were targeting the first responders who were rescuing people, my brother was one of them, he wasn't armed. In the absence of water, the bathrooms were an additional burden on us when relieving ourselves. Life is very fragile when people are unable to attend to their basic needs. We sank to a lamentable state, we began to grow weak, the filth began to accumulate. Our bodies were our prisons. They became very cumbersome. The situation grew even worse when the fuel ran out. We'd begun to cut off electricity from important wards to make it available for the intensive care ward and the premature babies. In the end, the fuel was on the brink of running out and we had to choose one over the other, intensive care or the neonatal incubators. It was a very difficult decision. It is one of the hardest moments, when you must literally cut a piece off your body so you can pass through a narrow gap, when it is your duty to decide who dies so another can live. In the end, the decision was made to concentrate the electricity on the neonatal unit, instead of the equipment for intensive care.

In mid-November, Deputy Minister for Health Dr Yusuf Abu al-Rish refused the Israeli army's demand to leave the hospital and meet with them, so Dr Marwan Abu Saada and Dr Muhammad Abu Salmiya went in his stead. In that meeting, the Israeli army ordered the total evacuation of the hospital. They said, verbatim: *You must evacuate the hospital, or we will tear it down it over your heads*. The complex was filled with thousands of people, including patients and their carers, displaced people, the medical teams. We requested ambulances so we could transport wounded patients who couldn't move, and we asked for specialized vehicles to transport the infants in their incubators. The Israeli army refused. The officer said to me: *We won't give you ambulances. Put them on your shoulders and get out of here*. Leaving in such a way would lead to the murder of the children and the wounded. On the following day, the occupation army allowed the premature infants to be transported in incubators. There were thirty-four premature babies; three died, the rest reached Egypt. Then the army repeated its threats to bomb the hospital over our heads. It was very painful; we didn't want to endanger people and families. Everyone who was able to walk left, which left more than 200 wounded who were unable to walk – one of whom was my brother – and we stayed with them. We went down into the basement levels for fear of the anticipated bombardment. We knew the Israelis to be capable of anything, so we took their threats absolutely seriously. We stayed there for a week, requesting ambulances to evacuate amputees and disabled patients, and the Israeli officer continued to refuse. A internal struggle tore me apart – between my brother, who needed someone to evacuate him from the hospital, and the other patients who didn't have anyone responsible for them. I was worried about my brother, so I readied him to leave, and then planned to return. A little girl close by, who was injured and couldn't move, screamed in terror, 'Don't leave us here alone!' In that moment, I utterly collapsed. I made up my mind to stay. I asked my brother to leave in a wheelchair with our neighbour, but he refused to go. I told him that I couldn't leave, I had to stay, I wouldn't abandon the patients. My brother replied, 'And I'm not leaving without you, we'll live together or die together.'

On 17 November, the occupying army gave us its final warning: *Leave tomorrow between seven in the morning and one in the afternoon, or be bombed without mercy*. We went out to them, the entire medical team approached the Israeli army. Seven doctors: the director of the hospital Muhammad Abu Salmiya, Marwan Abu Saada, Muataz Harara, Muhammad Eid, Jamal al-Harazin, Ahmad al-Wahidi and me. There were three female nurses with us. That was the entire remaining medical team. We said to them, 'We will not leave and we will not abandon our patients. We want ambulances so we can leave together. Apart from that, do whatever you want – kill us, bomb us, we will die with them. Go ahead and kill us. We will stay to the last moment, we're no better than them, we will die with our patients.' We said many things. I remember we also said, 'You have bombed hospitals and graveyards – we're no better than others. Do what you want, we will not leave our patients.'

48

What happened after that? They stormed the hospital. They didn't bomb it, but they did worse inside, engaging in indescribable barbarity. They dug holes here and there, they destroyed walls and equipment, they smashed up the only MRI machine in Gaza. At first, they put some guns they had brought next to it and began taking photographs. That was idiotic – no rational person could possibly imagine a metal weapon in an MRI room. They wanted to tell the world: *Look, we found weapons inside the hospital.* I witnessed them staging everything.

They stormed the empty buildings, dug up rooms, labs and basements. They reduced the hospital to rubble. We were saying to them, 'There's no one here!' They said they had intelligence fighters were inside. It was just a pretext, they would scream and shout and accuse us of hiding terrorists. Despite all their claims, despite all their digging, they didn't find a trace of anything they had claimed. They only found the gun belonging to the civil security that protected the hospital. There isn't a hospital in the world without police, there were no fighters among them. I am speaking now about the civilian police force for protecting a facility. The Israelis couldn't prove any theory they had alleged. I was there.

After they had finished ransacking, digging up and destroying the empty buildings, they entered the ones where the displaced and the patients were sheltering. All of a sudden, they blew the door open and rushed inside. They did it like they were in a film, they could have simply opened the door and walked in. I think the explosion came from a bomb, I'm not certain, but the noise was very powerful. Everyone was terrified. An army storming a hospital's intensive care ward with bombs! After that, they spread out and made us – the medical team and the displaced people – lie on the floor, while the patients, who could not move, stayed in their beds. They were looking for certain names, including the names of every person who had a connection with the Ministry of the Interior – according to them, every single government employee was a wanted person. That was most people! That order was madness, it proved they weren't looking for fighters, these people wanted to take everyone. They arrested all public sector workers, simply for being government employees. One patient had had both legs and his right hand amputated. He refused to give the Israeli officer his identity card, so the officer asked a soldier to come in. A heavily armed soldier came and took a scan of the patient's eye.* Two minutes later they arrested him and we found ourselves at an orgy of sadistic torture. They were beating a dismembered man on his stumps and on his wounds. Everyone was screaming, it was so horrific. They tortured us by torturing him in front of us, we were humiliated, and in the end they took him away.

They arrested the majority of people. They didn't discriminate! The torture we saw was beyond what anyone could believe a human being could commit. After they finished their arrests, the officer came up to me and said: *Come here. You a nurse?* I said, 'I am Doctor Khaled Abu Samra.' He took me to the second floor. We had three other floors. There was an entire floor for surgery. He made me go into one of the rooms and said: *We want you. We won't arrest you, we want a service from you so you can go back to your family. If you want to see them again, you must do what I tell you.* I was silent. He said: *We're going to go into every room, one by one, we'll blow open the locked rooms, and you're going in first.* I realized what was happening. They

* Author's note: The iris is scanned to recognize a person using AI. This scan is performed by the soldier directly, along with drones equipped with this speciality.

were going to use me as a human shield, so that if there was a room with a bomb or anything else inside, I would die instead of them. I was certain that we had no weapons. They put a gun to my head, beat me, struck me on the chest, hurled abuse at me. I said, 'I'll do what you want.' I went into the rooms, room after room, amid their abuse, and they were saying: *You'll die too if we find anyone here, all of you will die.*

On the fourth floor, there was a wind blowing. It was the beginning of winter, and when the door was opened it created a draught. I opened the door, went inside, and said there was no one there, so they followed me in and began searching. But suddenly, the draught slammed the door shut and there was a loud bang. They all dropped to the ground in fear and started yelling. I instantly froze. I thought their fear would make them lose their minds and they would shoot. Even now, that insult hasn't left me – being used as a human shield. In that moment, I realized how worthless our lives are to them. By the time we finished, we had spent four continuous hours touring the hospital. I was in the front. With their rifles in my side, I had to go first and encounter the first bullet or trigger the first mine, if there were any. In the end they found nothing. I was with them while they searched, and they couldn't find a shred of proof for any of the accusations they hurled out and presented as fact to the world. After four hours of being terrorized, being subject to violence and curses and beatings, after we had been to every single room, they let me go.

We remained under siege in our rooms, half under arrest, until 23 November. They used to torture the wounded patients in front of me. When the patients were in severe pain, they gave them morphine so they wouldn't pass out. They would torture and abuse them, making use of their wounds, and then give them morphine so they could torture them some more.

The Israeli army didn't stop their digging, our calls to the media to evacuate the wounded continued, and we remained at an impasse, because we doctors would never leave without our patients. Eventually, the Israelis agreed to evacuate in coordination with the Red Crescent and the UN, and we were asked how we would evacuate and how many ambulances we needed. We replied that we had 170 wounded requiring a minimum of 70 ambulances, but they only brought 14 ambulances and 2 minibuses and said: *This is all there is, there's nothing else*. We didn't know how we would transport the wounded. We crammed them in side by side, pushing one amputee to the side and squeezing another amputee right up to him. That's how we arranged the remnants of human bodies, like we were packing suitcases.

On 23 November, we left al-Shifa Hospital. The hospital was still under siege. Al-Wahda Street and the surrounding areas were strewn with tanks. I left with my brother in a minibus that was supposed to seat twenty, but all together, one on top of another, there were more than fifty of us. Most of the passengers were wounded and injured. Simply driving over the cratered streets heralded a torture spree, with open wounds dripping blood. There were UN vehicles in front of us and a military jeep behind us. We had to head south – these were the orders of the Israeli army. We asked to go north, but they refused. They forced us south, it was all planned.

Along the way, the cars drove through corpses. This is no exaggeration, there were corpses everywhere, left lying in piles. Gaza had become a city of the murdered, a city of ghosts. At al-Shuja'iyya junction, bodies were strewn over the ground like a carpet, not an inch between them. Women and men, children, corpses. The army saw them, the soldiers were walking through the streets and stepping over them, as though these human bodies didn't exist.

When we reached the corridor separating north and south, we were stopped. They had set up a checkpoint on the site of Netzarim, a settlement that they had evicted twenty years earlier.* I felt as though my head wasn't in place on top of my body, I felt dizzy. Shattered, I couldn't focus. We were crying – all of us men – crammed into the bus, we were all sobbing.

It was exactly half past twelve when we reached the frightening checkpoint. And so the waiting commenced. Nine out of every ten people coming from the hospital were in a critical condition and on the brink of death. Nevertheless, they left us to wait from half past twelve until eight o'clock in the evening. Eight hours, with all these bodies crammed into buses and ambulances, forbidden to move or get out. Some elderly people urinated on their seats.

At eight o'clock, they sent us into a huge yard. They had swept it, and I wondered if human bodies had been swept away too. Then they made us and the ambulances go round the yard in a circle like a military parade. Searchlights were directed at us, we went round and round, fourteen ambulances and both buses too. Then they carried out a search of every ambulance, and each search took half an hour. They were saying that there were wounded people escaping the Baptist Hospital and they were wanted. They were hunting injured people fleeing a massacre. They were hunting survivors of a massacre in

---

* The inhabitants of Netzarim, an Israeli settlement in the Gaza strip, were evicted by the Israeli government in August 2005 as part of Ariel Sharon's Disengagement Plan Implementation Law, a unilateral disengagement plan.

order to kill them. I will never forget that checkpoint, the Netzarim Corridor.

MUHAMMAD FADI SALEH
25 years old
North Gaza

I was standing in front of my house when the bomb fell at the end of the street. I went out to see what was happening but I couldn't get close. Then they bombed a second time, I was about a hundred metres away, the explosion was intense. I went flying and slammed into the ground hard. I felt shrapnel piercing my body everywhere. I tried to move but I couldn't. I was surrounded by corpses and wounded people, and someone nearby tried to help me, but there were many wounded and even more martyrs. A single ambulance arrived, it took us all. Seeing how many wounded there were, they put me in the back with a few others.

We arrived at Kamal Adwan Hospital, everything was running out: medicine, anaesthetic, vital medical equipment. They couldn't even diagnose me. I was suffering from complete paralysis in my legs. After a while, I was transferred to the Indonesian Hospital, but there things were even worse. No electricity, no generators, no possibility of running the necessary imaging. After many hours of waiting, I and a few other wounded were able to have a CT scan. It showed there was pressure on my spinal column, but the doctors couldn't explain the paralysis.

They moved me to al-Shifa Hospital. I was completely exhausted and bleeding heavily. I couldn't speak, the place was crowded with wounded and there was blood everywhere. There wasn't a bed for me in intensive care, so they put me on a mattress on the floor in between the other wounded people. Corpses and limbs were scattered about next to me. Because of internal bleeding in my chest, they performed an emergency procedure on me on that mattress, then they put a cannula in my chest to drain the blood. After that they admitted me to the hospital, on the condition that I stay on the same mattress. I couldn't understand what was happening, or why my body wouldn't respond to me.

The following day, the doctors requested an MRI but it wasn't available. They kept trying to understand the reason for the paralysis, but it was no use. I lost control over my bladder and my bowels, they fitted me with a catheter. On the fourth day, the Israelis dropped leaflets demanding the evacuation of the hospital, and they bombed the maternity ward where the newborns and premature babies were. I was there in that moment, I couldn't move. I was overwhelmed with fear, the bombing was continuous. I was frightened the Israeli soldiers would enter and kill us, as we had heard about instances of mass cleansing.

After hours of horror, my uncle came. I was shouting at him to leave me, I didn't want to be a burden on him. But my uncle insisted on taking me out of the hospital. We knew that the hospital was preparing for evacuation, and the Israelis were getting closer. My uncle pushed me in a wheelchair under rain and bombardment. After half an hour of walking, we found a car and it took me home. My family was afraid, everyone around me was panicking. I was sick, my temperature went up, my body was burning up, no one knew what was wrong with me. We tried to call the doctors, but couldn't get through. I stayed like that for days, being moved from house to house, we were continually being displaced by bombing.

After fifteen days of suffering, the Red Cross came to Kamal Adwan Hospital to evacuate the patients. There was a ceasefire,* and on the fourth day of the ceasefire, we

---

* Author's note: On 24 November 2023, a temporary ceasefire came into effect between Israel and Hamas in the Gaza Strip. It lasted four days. This agreement was reached through Qatari mediation, and stipulated a ceasefire and exchange of prisoners, whereby Hamas released 50 hostages in exchange for the release of 150 Palestinian captives. The agreement also allowed humanitarian aid into the Gaza Strip for the duration of the ceasefire.

were evacuated with the Red Cross.*

I arrived at Nasser Hospital on 26 November, there were not enough beds and there was no space for me. After six or seven hours of searching, they finally put me in a bed. By that time I was utterly exhausted and the pain was tearing me apart, I was in urgent need of painkillers, but there weren't any. The pain was horrific. As days went by, I came down with a clot on the foot as result of not moving – or strictly speaking, because of my inability to move. That clot was a confirmation that my condition was getting worse, and I began to feel I was relapsing. My health regressed noticeably.

My family tried to take me out of Gaza so I could receive treatment abroad – they could see my situation deteriorating day by day – but they couldn't. I stayed in Nasser Hospital without any treatment to speak of. The most they offered me was antibiotics. There was no effective medical intervention, no rehabilitation, no physiotherapy. As the days went by, I could feel my life fading away, especially as the bombing was still going on. I believed I would die in my bed, paralysed and helpless.

The doctors told me I was suffering some kind of wound in my spinal cord, but what could they do in light of what was going on? The bombing was non-stop, bodies were scattered all around us, the hospital was running out of everything. We were living in among the wounded and the sick and the scattered corpses. Everything indicated that I wouldn't survive.

Then the Israeli army came and ordered an evacuation of this hospital as well. They said to leave the patients who couldn't walk – I was one of them – without any carers. My mother refused to leave me alone to their mercy. She stayed with me, repositioning me and caring for

* This is an example of the non-linearity of the narratives. At this
  point, Muhammad has been readmitted to Kamal Adwan Hospital.

57

my wounds. She refused to leave – in her eyes, leaving me would mean my death. Ulcers began to appear on my back from not moving. But in the end, they ordered the carers to leave, otherwise they would kill them. I forced my mother to leave the hospital. She was the last to go. She tried to evade them, but five soldiers with several guns surrounded her with, and she was cut off from me for days.

During those days, I didn't move at all. I was completely helpless. The soldiers were occupying the hospital, they beat the wounded violently and they insulted us all. I was one of the ones beaten and humiliated. An Israeli soldier approached me and I told him calmly that I was just a paralysed patient, I couldn't move. But not satisfied with merely beating me, he threatened me with rape. He grinned nastily and began to shake my bed violently, as if he was acting out a sex scene, yanking the bed back and forth, making sounds like he was enjoying it. He kept looking at me and demanding that I open my eyes. He kept on insulting me and humiliating me. His face was full of mockery and glee, and I couldn't do a thing about it. I could only close my eyes, trying to escape this nightmare with my mind.

I was there, in the heart of hell, when the Israelis stormed the hospital with their trained dogs and loosed them on us. The zannana was hovering over us, threatening us with more bombing. All the while, bodily and verbal abuse – it was a mix of sexual harassment, humiliation and continuous threats of rape. They moved us in our beds and took us to the outside courtyard where they carried on the beating and torture. They beat me several times, on my head and face and chest, with a violence I can't describe. I felt like a tattered rag at their hands.

They took us to a place crowded with the wounded,

people with limbs cut off, those on the verge of death. They tied my hands, put a blindfold over my eyes, and began to interrogate me while continuing their violent beatings. They beat me on the head with a stick, over and over and over, until I thought I was going to pass out. Then they left us there. We were all moaning in pain. Then doctors from their side came in to assess us. But they left us there. Our wounds were open, blood and urine and faeces were smeared all over the place. We existed in a state that can only be described as slow death, powerless to move or to speak, other than by groans, which gradually got fainter.

An Israeli solder came back and told me to stand up. I told him I was paralysed. He lifted me up then threw me on the ground, again and again, until I began to black out. My wounds began to reopen and stream with blood. In that moment, my only thought was wondering how I was going to die. I hoped it would be quick. I was seeking a way out of it all, and then they brought the dogs in. I thought they were going to eat us. That day, a cat came in and sat on top of a man next to me. It began to eat his severed foot. They were watching, they enjoyed looking at us while we were dying.

They left us there, in that living nightmare, until finally they withdrew. I am still traumatized. Paramedics arrived and moved me to a camp without any medical care or treatment. No medicine, no painkillers, not even a minimum of concern. I was living in expectation of a slow death, as there wasn't any means of treatment or relief from the pain. The doctors told me I needed to leave Gaza to receive treatment, but I was detained because Israeli control of the crossings prevents young men from travelling. Stuck between life and death, I am moved from camp to camp, while my family are still in the north, living another nightmare.

I don't ask the impossible. I don't ask to walk again. All I want is a quick end to this torment. But I am stuck here, in Rafah Camp, where medicine is rare and costs a fantastical amount. All I can do now is wait to die, slowly, between life and death, living deaths, without any path of escape.

NADA EISA AYYAASH
40 years old
Jabalia Camp

I was born in exile and I came back to Gaza. I got married and made a small family that lived in the heart of a large extended family in Jabalia Camp. Brothers and sisters, grandparents and grandchildren, parents and children all gathered together in one large building. I worked as a teacher in the relief agency UNRWA. I stayed so I could serve Palestinian refugees through my work, aside from being active in international humanitarian, development and relief community organizations. I wasn't a member of any faction or party, I have no connection to Hamas, I don't care about the Palestinian Authority. All I wanted, like other Palestinians, was to live in safety.

I achieved my dream and was content to be helping my country's children, but this didn't mean that we were living in paradise. War was a background to our lives; I have lived through perhaps four of them. But those were wars where the bombing came in instalments, death and destruction came unhurriedly. They weren't genocide. We always had an emergency bag packed with a unique mix of memories and necessities so we could grab it and leave as soon as there was any bombing. In the last war, the Israelis bombed my neighbour's house, which wasn't harbouring Hamas men. And I know that they know everything about us, large or small. Cameras, intelligence, drones. So, when the current war began, I said, 'We're not leaving, we'll stay in our home.' That is what my immediate and extended family decided – it would be no different from the previous times. But those were wars, whereas what is happening to us now... you need to be insane just to imagine it, then believe it.

On the morning of 10 October 2023, at half past ten, the Israelis bombed the family home. It was no help to us that our house in Baraka Abu Rashid in Jabalia Camp was located next to one of the UNRWA schools, which was then crammed full of displaced people. They knew everything, so two missiles falling right inside our building was completely unexpected. That morning, I hadn't been in the best state. I had a high temperature and felt absolutely drained, the fever had a habit of making me hallucinate and faint. For some reason, I told my husband, Hussam Ahmed, 42 years old, to take both children – Ala who is 8, and Muhammad who is 5 – to say hello to their grandparents and their aunts and uncles. No! I don't think I had any premonition of what was going to happen, I don't think the fever sharpened my instincts or revealed the unknown. All there was to it was that this was something I liked my children to do, to keep up a connection with the rest of the family.

They bombed us while my children were gone, just five minutes after they left. Two missiles, the Shafat kind.* At first I didn't hear the noise, you don't when you're targeted to die. I couldn't understand anything, I was flying, full of fever, in a hideous nightmare, only woken by a violent crash into the earth, by horrendous rubble falling on top of me and burying me under the debris. I couldn't feel anything in the moment. In the two seconds I went flying, those two missiles were sucking up the souls of twenty-five people from my husband's family. Grandmother,

* Author's note: Shafat can be translated as suction in English. This is the common Palestinian term for a vacuum bomb, i.e. a thermobaric bomb, a non-nuclear bomb that possesses an immense destructive force. Thermobaric bombs ignite a cloud of combustible fragments and 'suck up' the surrounding oxygen, generating an intense explosion, usually producing a blast wave of much longer duration compared to conventional explosives.

uncles and aunts, their children, all of them gone. In that insanity, it took no more than two seconds to suck up twenty-five souls. By some miracle I still don't understand, my husband survived, both my children survived and I survived.

The family disappeared in the blink of an eye, everyone was under the rubble, and the bodies were brought out one by one. While I was under the rubble, I heard my daughter Ala screaming, she was calling for her father. And not just her, I heard screaming coming from everywhere, I heard my husband's father calling out for my daughter, looking for her, and the ground all around us was on fire, as if we were at the centre of a stone fireplace. Later, I learned that Ala's grandfather followed his granddaughter's voice until he found her, and then he dug with his fingernails to give her some air. My little daughter almost suffocated to death. She was almost buried alive. I learned later that they dug her out with their bare hands, with their fingers and nails and skin. They didn't have any machines or tools, they did it by instinct which grew and became a miracle, and they succeeded, and they brought Ala out with an iron bar through her leg.

All that time, I was still under the rubble, I could hear them shouting in search of the living. I didn't think I was alive, so I didn't bother replying. I was aware that I had died, that I was leaving this world, and that everything taking place around me was nothing but the periphery of the path to the other world. In any case, it would have made no difference if I hadn't had this awareness – it felt as though I'd lost the ability to speak, or rather I'd forgotten how to, as if I had never learned it in the first place. I didn't scream in horror or in pain, I didn't breathe a word. Just my hand poked out from the wreckage, like an early plant coming out of the ground, so they knew where I was. It was Ala's grandfather who saw it, and he hurried over and began to dig around me to get me out. That's when my mouth regained its memory and I began to scream. Horrific agony, pain I can't describe, but I didn't know exactly where it was coming from. My body was like tattered shreds of meat, as if I was being flayed from head to foot. This is the best I can do to describe my state in that moment: I was entirely pain. This didn't mean I knew I was alive as, truly, pain of that kind is part of death.

At the Indonesian Hospital, I discovered that I wasn't dead yet. They took me there after they brought me out, and there, amid all the sounds of pain and moaning and horror, I made out the sound of Ala screaming, and her voice was a token of life. In hospital – they discharged me quickly despite my injuries, my burns, the accumulation of gashes in my flesh over my bones – I learned what had happened to the family. We were the only survivors, and now my husband had to bury twenty-five members of his family. And the bombs never quietened.

The Israelis throw their warning leaflets and bomb immediately. They throw their leaflets and don't give people time to pack their things and count heads and leave with anything more than the clothes on their backs. They throw leaflets like they're using them as proof against us: *We warned you!* And that's just a lie, like all their lies which the world believes, and which I want to believe too, so I can live. A huge lie, yes, because they bomb straight after throwing the leaflets, they bomb without discrimination, they bomb schools and hospitals and camps and places where the displaced are sheltering. All this, and the ground invasion still hadn't started yet.

Our grandparents have lived through war, our parents have lived through it, we and our children have lived through it. There is a history of martyrs in our family, my husband's sister is a widow, her husband was a martyr, he was killed in the 2008 war, there's nothing new in this. But that situation wasn't the same, it wasn't like this. We have been prisoners in Gaza for years. In the twenty years I have been living in the Strip, I have experienced death. Death comes and death goes, four wars perhaps, or five, I can't keep count. But it never reached the level of genocide. I have endured life here because it is my home, and because I live with my wider family. And I belong to the upper middle class and suffer even so, so what about others? Life in prison is very hard – its challenges are no easier even when it is a larger prison than normal. I have lived through several wars. We leave one war only to enter into another, not including the occasional air raids that Israel launches from time to time. But everything before seems like silly games to me, now. Every year, there was Israeli hostility, there was violent bombardment, there was indiscriminate murder, but this time things are different.

As days passed, my leg became inflamed because of infection. There were so many wounds, parts of my flesh were gone. I began to feel my body declining. I suffered from vaginal bleeding, and it lasted for a long time. I spoke with the doctors to understand the reason for it, they all said they didn't know what was happening, they said the Israelis were using new, prohibited weapons. The poisons and chemicals dropped onto us were causing strange symptoms. It wasn't just blood, I would see fleshy, bloody lumps coming out of me. I would feel something inside my abdomen detach and then come out, and after that my periods stopped. Perhaps the poison penetrated my skin, or perhaps my wounds absorbed it. I suffered from inflammation in every part of my body, and my wounds wouldn't heal. This is the state of my body. As for what is going on inside my psyche, I can't describe it. Words will never come to my aid. I cry all the time, we weep twenty-four hours a day, everyone I love has gone. Innocent children, splendid as roses, evaporated in an instant. Babies with milk still on their lips, suffocated to death by chemicals. A grandmother as gentle as a breeze in spring – whenever one of them asked why I didn't leave Gaza, I would immediately reply, 'I would never leave such a lovely grandmother.' She is now dead.

We moved north, to my family home in al-Saftawy, and I was in a wheelchair. We moved under bombardment, but however intense the bombing, it wasn't enough to quieten my agony. I had no medical treatment apart from oral antibiotics, and I couldn't move. My daughter needed oxygen after suffocating under the debris, and my husband was still trying to bury his dead. My disabled father who suffers from weak vision and many illnesses, my elderly mother, my brother with his seven children, my sister and her husband, my daughter and I. The insanity wasn't more than two days behind us. Just two days. Two days after the massacre, on 12 October, the Israelis dropped their leaflets on us. It was horror, it was the Day of Hashr* that crept in like a thief when the family was sleeping, these moments when the family gathered up whichever of their children they could find, then returned afterwards to pick up whoever had been forgotten. My sister's husband carried my daughter Ala, and he put me in his car with the wheelchair.

The small amount of petrol we still had left, and my brother-in-law's decision to leave straight away no matter what, before they closed Salah al-Din Road – these

* In Islamic eschatology, the Day of Hashr, or Day of Gathering, is when all creatures are resurrected and gathered for Judgement Day. There are different interpretations of what will occur, but it is believed that the gathering will be painful and overwhelming.

were the two reasons for our survival. We left the rest of my family, and every jolt of the car, or rather every one of its knife thrusts, generated indescribable pain. My body was all knives, and every moment those knives carved deeper into my flesh, nerves and bones. We headed south of Wadi Gaza – these were the Israelis' orders. They expelled us, coming from the air to finish off the wounded and the survivors from the massacres they had committed before, then they pursued us to our new site of displacement. A deliberate decision of genocide, as if they intended that no one would be left. At last, we reached Nuseirat, and ten minutes after we arrived, they closed Salah al-Din Road. Whoever was left in the other part, north of the wadi, was now trapped.

In Nuseirat Camp, my grandfather lived in an abandoned house. A ruin with no bathroom or water. My wounds were open, Ala was sobbing from pain and Muhammad said, 'This is a house of demons, I am not happy.' He was 5 years old, and now capable of speaking while staring with glazed eyes: 'I am not happy.' I called my husband and asked him to come to us, he told me he hadn't finished bringing out his family's bodies yet. It would take – he predicted – another seven days to take out all the bodies and bury them, apart from his sister, whose body was torn into pieces. Because we wanted to see him so badly, and because he wanted to be reassured about us, he would come and then go back to the site of the massacre. He knew no peace as long as his family members were unburied. Afterwards, he suggested that we move to his house. It wouldn't be any better, but there was no choice. There, we would be squashed into one house with dozens of people, and once again we would have no water. Without water, we couldn't bathe or use the toilet, without water I couldn't care for my wounds.

But it wasn't just me, everyone was in the same situation, every person had their injuries and problems. At this point, the ground operation began in Jabalia.

That day was 3 December. At al-Aqsa Hospital, the doctor took one look at my red, swollen leg and said bluntly, 'You need an operation.' Then he added, 'We can't do it, I'll make do with sterilizing your wounds.' 'Can I have some antibiotics?' 'We don't have any.' The hospital was filled with others, full to bursting with the displaced and the wounded, infection and smells. Naama, my husband's sister, was killed in a bombing along with her seven children, she left behind a baby daughter. The number of our dead rose to – thirty-three? The polluted water had its effect on me, I came down with poisoning, I couldn't stop vomiting. And the bombing reached everywhere: the civilian police, hospitals, clinics, the Red Cross, Doctors Without Borders. We no longer had any relief aid or medical services, now there was no care of any kind for the injured or the sick, not even medicine to stop my vomiting. The doctor told my husband, 'You see the water in tinned food? A tin of beans, for example?' They juiced a lemon and said, 'She should drink that.' That was his prescription! My husband said he was prepared to pay for medicines, the doctor stressed that there weren't any available. 'Don't torture yourselves.'

This time, we went to my aunt's house in al-Zawayda. My family had gone ahead of me and we stayed together in a single room, fourteen people including my disabled father. No bed, no blanket, no electricity, no phone line, no internet. I was sleeping on the floor together with my pain, and my husband spent every day walking an hour there and an hour back to come and reassure himself about us. Then we were displaced to Rafah.

In Rafah the situation was no better. There were fifty

displaced people in the apartment, or maybe eighty. They put me in an apartment because I was injured. One bathroom for fifty people, or eighty. They provided us with some tins of food and some polluted drinking water. When water is scarce, eating and drinking become very anxiety-provoking. How will I go to the toilet? How will I clean myself? I was starving to the point of fainting, I was thirsty to the point of drying out and many people, including my son Muhammad, came down with hepatitis. The water was contaminated, the place was contaminated, the air was contaminated. All around me were skeleton shapes, my son and daughter among them. The people of Rafah helped a lot, but what could they do to stop our suffering, or even alleviate it? The pain was intense, the tragedy was huge. I feel that talking about it, repeating the same vocabulary, will trivialize the whole issue, but what can be done? Where would a new language come from? What I was most ashamed of was the screaming, my screaming – that men and women I didn't know could hear my screams. I was utterly humiliated but I couldn't control it, my agony never calmed, my injuries never healed. I felt naked in front of them – the sounds that came out of me despite myself made me feel I was naked in front of fifty people, or maybe eighty. Shame, huge shame, all made worse by my smell.

We were displaced five times in four months. I look at my sick daughter, at my burns, at my festering wounds, at my infected leg, at all of us piled up like hunks of meat, and I keep crying and praying to God that He will have mercy on me and not leave me alive to the following day. I think of my son's eloquence: *I am not happy*. He is still 5, but his hair is white. A white haired child! The force of the blast sent him flying like one of his superheroes he used to watch on the cartoon channel, and he landed on

69

the roof of an empty building. They found him standing upright, repeating: 'The world is red, the world is red.' He still says it today: *the world is red*.

We stayed in Rafah for ten days. The prices were outrageous, we didn't have cash or bank cards with us, and everyone was hungry. Three quarters of Gaza's people were gathered in Rafah. You would walk in the streets and not see anything but the hungry, the sick, amputees, half-bodies wandering aimlessly in wheelchairs. A nightmare, a mythical plague, a great suffocation from the smells – the smell of our infected wounds, along with the smell of corpses rotting under the rubble. The smell of death and decay was everywhere. The half-dead and the half-alive lived side by side. We saw our bodies decomposing under our very eyes, we saw maggots coming out from the wounds. That stench! Bodies, infection, piled-up garbage mixed with human flesh.

Two children survived the family massacre: a girl of a year and a half, and a 14-year-old boy, orphans left behind by my husband's two sisters. Now they are our children.

I don't know which is worse, the psychological pain or the physical pain, but I have noticed something strange: many times, the pain of the body dominates the psychological pain, as if my open wounds are helping me forget the grief. Grief, in a hell like this, is an inappropriate luxury. Then I find myself unable to sleep for four days, pictures of the massacre won't leave me alone: I see family members suffocated under the rubble, their bodies still whole. This is what a shafat bomb does, it has some kind of relationship with air pressure, it rips up people's organs and they disintegrate on the inside, but from the outside, the body remains intact. I see them all, here in my head – children, young people, old people. They were good and kind, they loved life even though it was hard.

70

I see them, and I can't get rid of the smell. I haven't said anything at all – all that I've told you and I haven't said *anything* yet. There are many details, hideous details, fatal details, but I'm not capable of telling them. My past life I will call my first life. It took me forty years to establish it, and now I must start again from zero, from less than zero, to establish a second life that I know nothing about. All I know is I must go on, for the sake of my children.

SHAIMAA NAJI
21 years old
Jabalia

Ever since opening my eyes onto the world and feeling all the wars taking place in this city, since childhood, I have come to expect tragedies like this. But this time it's not a war. When I hear someone saying 'the war in Gaza', I feel angry and crushed.

We used to live like normal people, like any other normal family. My brother and I studied software engineering, I graduated with a diploma and was one of the top of my class. I worked and studied at the same time, and I specialized in website design. My office was next to al-Shifa Hospital. Actually, I used to take a photo of the road every day – for some reason, I imagined that these pictures would become a memory. I was gripped by a sense that everything was going to go away, I used to take photos without stopping – perhaps – to expel the bad visions from my head.

On 7 October, I was planning to go to university. I live in my family building where my uncles live with their children and grandchildren. I was praying the fajr prayer when I heard the rockets. At first, I thought it was just thunder before the rain. I opened the window and then I saw rockets filling the sky. We stayed at home and refused to leave, even after they bombed our neighbourhood. My uncles took their families and left, but my family stayed at home. Everywhere in Gaza is dangerous, there is no safe place, so we decided to stay put in our house and not go outside. We weren't frightened. We committed our souls to God and said what will be, will be. Our relatives were calling us and asking us to go, and despite the bombing all around us every day, I remember telling my uncle, 'I will not leave, I will die in my home.'

On 22 October, my grandmother came to see my father. She lived far away and my uncles were displaced to her house. Under intense bombardment, she came to see her son. My grandmother wept as she begged him to leave, but he was laughing, trying to make light of what was happening. My aunt came too, to convince him to leave and go to her house. They were very close, and she had a word alone with him. My family loved each another. We would eat dinner under continual bombing. Eventually, my father was convinced to leave – specifically, after he heard that many of his friends had died. But he said, 'I'll go out by myself, and you all go to dar sidkum.'* We wouldn't do it. We left all at once and went with him.

My aunt's house overlooked an avenue. That night, while we were staying awake in the room, I was trying to make them laugh and then went out onto the balcony to get some fresh air, only to be surprised to find a zannana right in front of me. It was watching us. At first I thought that it was a missile fired remotely and it occurred to me to take a picture, but I suddenly noticed it was a reconnaissance drone, and it had in fact been taking pictures of us. I hurried back inside, heavy-hearted. Before long, we heard it shoot. We realized later that it was scoping the place out. My father was a target. These drones, quadcopters, can shoot or detonate themselves. As if murdering in person isn't enough, they've brought us mechanical murder in the form of drones. We saw light coming from the bombed areas, someone shouted, 'That's phosphorus,' but phosphorus doesn't glow – I know it, I'm familiar with it. In the past, they often hit us with phosphorus, and with other bombs I can't remember the names of any more. I got to be afraid of dying from cancer because of how

* Dar sidkum – your grandfather's house.

much phosphorus I inhaled in my childhood. I have vivid memories of choking fits.

We went into the living room, horrified. My father began joking around with us, feigning humour. I looked into his eyes. Behind his simulated calm, I noticed deep anxiety in his face. The sound of bombing rose all around us, and we were behaving as if nothing was happening. I really don't know why we ignored the drone incident and decided to stay. It was twenty past midnight when my father asked us all to go to bed, and he in turn went to another room. I saw him close the door. That was the last time. I never saw my father again after that.

We were all secretly frightened, and everyone was silent. We fell asleep at once. Or so I thought – my sister would tell me later that she couldn't sleep and so she actually saw everything herself.

I woke to a sea of fire and the sound of explosions. We were on the third floor of a five-storey building. There we were, and all five floors were collapsing. Eleven people died immediately, including my father.

The house was burning, waves of flame rose and fell. My brain couldn't interpret what it was seeing, it was like being in a dream. I felt my head explode, for a moment I didn't realize what had happened to me. All this took place in seconds. I noticed a hand trying to get hold of me – as soon as I touched it, the rubble sent me sliding. I went rolling with the rocks while the floor above came down and turned into wreckage and debris. The hand belonged to my aunt, who was martyred at that moment. I think she touched me before she died. She was trying to save me, or perhaps she was trying to cling to me, and while I was sliding on the rubble I crashed into a rock and was sent flying along with the rubble. They said that I flew about thirty metres. I had completely blacked out by then.

When I opened my eyes, I thought I was dead. I blacked out again, only to find myself buried in the wreckage, my head in the air and my body under the debris. The world all around was dark, and I was far away from everyone else. People had gathered to help, and I was screaming, 'Hey! Over here, help!' I shouted and screamed to get them to hear me. People were screaming – everyone was screaming! I felt a terrible pain in my body. Suddenly, I saw my hand come out from under the rubble, covered in blood and dust. My limbs were moving independently, involuntarily. I could hear ambulances, there was dust covering everything, everything around me was black, I couldn't breathe. My body was black, black covered me, even my eyes. I saw women coming out from under the rubble, they looked like dead people coming out of graves. I screamed, 'Hey, everyone, I'm over here... I'm alive!' They were too far away, no one could hear me. I saw my sister trying to raise her body from under the rubble and I shouted, 'Raghad... Raghad, my sister! Get her out.' I was shouting with all my might, until they heard me and came and brought us out, me and my sister.

I saw burned bodies scattered all over. They flung a blanket over me, I refused it. I told them I was suffocating. They wanted to cover up my body, but I screamed, 'Leave me alone.' Finally they pulled me out, and my body was full of injuries and shrapnel. Even now, there is shrapnel in my body. The missiles contain a substance that turns into small black dots that leave marks on the body, a strange chemical I don't know, they say it's toxic. The bodies were covered in spots, and there are still traces of that substance in my body. While they were bringing me out, I saw them bring out a cat that had been completely burned. It was black, like coal.

My cousin picked me up and put me in an ambulance.

All the roads were full of holes because of the bombardment, the ambulance jolted over the holes, jolting me at the same time. I was screaming in pain. In fear, I yelled, 'I want Abi and Ummi, I want my brothers and sisters.' The pain was horrendous. My teeth were chattering with horror, and my knees were shaking. The hospital was full of injured people and the people accompanying them, displaced people were sleeping in the corridors. I was screaming in pain; everyone around me was screaming in pain. The doctors were roaming around us, powerless, all the sick were begging for painkillers, there was a lack of medical equipment, there was no more anaesthetic. The place was overflowing with dead as well, I heard the doctors pointing near to me, 'This woman's dead, and that one, take them away.' I couldn't move my head to see the dead people that he was pointing at. A patient right opposite me outside the door asked for some water, he was waiting his turn for dialysis, so I understood, but it was five days late because of the electricity being cut off. They brought him a cup of water, and as soon as the water wet his lips, the cup fell from his hand and he died. I learned that there was also a lack of shrouds. They moved me to another bed, away from the dead woman lying next to me. I couldn't move, I was screaming, my pain reached up to the sky. The following day, my aunt's husband came and discharged me from the hospital, there was no treatment they could offer me. He took me, my sister and a cousin along with us, to my grandfather's house.* Our injuries weren't fatal, and there was no point us staying in hospital.

* As mentioned later in the 'Note on Translation', it was impractical to translate family relationships in full, although Arabic specifies whether aunts and uncles are on the maternal or paternal side. In this instance, the uncle in question is an uncle by marriage on the maternal side. He picked up the witness, her sister and a paternal cousin and took them all to the house of the witness's maternal grandfather. I note this to demonstrate the intricacy of family connections, and to underline the devastation that occurs when this tight-knit fabric is ripped.

My aunt's husband said goodbye and left. He died soon after.

My grandfather's house is in Mashrou' Beit Lahia. The bombs never fell quiet. All of Gaza began to live according to the rhythm of destruction. The features of the place changed from one hour to the next, there was no more asking about the dead, and we began only asking after people who were left alive. My aunt put me on a chair and began to clean me. Dirt and grit came out of my body, black blood flowed out of my wounds with the water. My hair is very long and odd things were embedded in it, like metal wires. I looked at my body for the first time after the explosion. It had injuries I could never have imagined. I burst into sobs! It was only at that moment I realized I was still breathing.

Our family was split up between hospitals. My mother stayed in the Indonesian Hospital, one leg was amputated and the other was in danger. My sister, who was in the same hospital, had a fractured pelvis. My third sister had a fracture in her leg and an injury in her eye. The were so many wounded and not enough doctors or medical equipment, so the doctors in the hospital asked us to choose between treating the leg and treating the eye. She had to decide which body part to give up in order to save the other. In the hospital, there was no plaster of Paris or platinum plates to set the bone, and her leg stayed like that, without treatment. Now she can't walk very well.

My father's body was in Kamal Adwan Hospital. They hid the news of his death from me at first. When my brother, who was accompanying my mother in the hospital, called to check on me, I asked him, 'Was Abi killed?' But he had got ahead of me and asked me about my brother Suhaib's clothes. I answered, 'Yes, he was wearing olive-green pyjamas.' He said, 'Well, your brother was martyred along with your cousin, and we have buried him.' I imagined Suhaib's face at once. They had only been able to recognize him from his clothes. Was his face disfigured to such an extent? My little brother, my darling Suhaib, had been completely burned. Blackened to coal. I was choking on my tears and kept asking, begging, 'Was our father martyred?' He replied, 'Yes.' Then I blacked out.

Every day, under bombardment and in among rubble and destruction, I would go to visit my mother in the Indonesian Hospital. I was still limping at that point. The place changed terrifyingly, everything had become different. My mother was traumatized after regaining consciousness to find herself without a leg. She can no longer walk, still. Sometimes I would go to sleep on the floor next to my mother's bed. My sister was in the same hospital, but in another ward that treated fractures. My wounds healed slowly, but the shrapnel stayed lodged in my body. Despite the pain, my wounds are nothing compared to the suffering of others. I walk for two minutes and stop, I move extremely slowly, even going to the bathroom can be tough. Even so, in the end I decided to not go back to my grandfather's house, which had filled up with displaced people, and instead to stay in the hospital with my mother and my sister. I said to myself, 'We'll all die together or live together.' I brought my sisters and we all began staying there, beside my mother. My two sisters and I would sleep on the floor, while my mother and my sister with the broken pelvis slept on the bed. My powerful grandmother, who was over 60, used to bring us whatever food she had. She would wash our clothes, and at last she would flood us with prayers.

The siege of the Indonesian Hospital began in November. We heard tanks at the gates, and it became forbidden to enter or leave. We spent five days under siege. I saw piles of dead bodies rising around the hospital. Where did all these murdered people come from? I saw cats and dogs tearing at corpses, flies hovering over the dead. We were choked by the stench of blood. I lived through this horror for five days, without water or electricity. Then they said that besieged people could leave. People rushed to flee, they were pushing and scrambling like it was Judgement Day. They left without a single glance at each other.

The patients and the displaced left together, and then only 180 people were left in the hospital, people who couldn't leave because their health was too bad. Me, my mother and sisters were among them. I couldn't leave with my mother and three sisters – not when my mother and one of my sisters couldn't move at all. We stayed on the second floor of the hospital, the window glass was broken because of the bombing, only the curtains separated us from the outside. Anyone trying to open the curtain was shot instantly. We were imprisoned where we sat. The sound of explosions and the scattering of shrapnel never stopped; the piles of bodies around the hospital rose continually. I was so intensely frightened for my family that I would take my mother and sisters into the corridors to sleep. The food ran out, there was nothing left but a single box of chocolates that we fed one at a time to the children. There were lots of hungry children. The water ran out as well. I saw maggots crawling out of my mother's amputated leg. I saw her bone sticking out. She was getting worse and worse and I would take hold of her leg and try to clean the wound. We kept sleeping in the corridors. The bombing all around us never stopped.

On 20 November, they bombed the third floor. We saw the surrounding towers swaying before our eyes, as if the world was collapsing. We fled the second floor and went with the other patients to the underground levels. I felt the shrapnel flame up inside my body. We were terrified.

In the basement, we found a large room where we could hide from the bombs. I thought that I would be buried underneath the rubble this time. The room was filled with rubbish, and we decided to clean it, despite our terror. We spent a whole day cleaning. We gathered up the filth but we couldn't take it outside – we were too frightened, the tank guns were aimed at the doors. The smell that day was so disgusting, I'll never forget it for the rest of my life. That same day we found a stale bread roll. We shared it between six people. That was our food for a whole day. Then the electricity was cut off after they bombed the generator, so we were plunged into pitch black. We tried – unsuccessfully – to calm the children.

The sound of tanks gradually got louder, and in fact they came right up to the doors of the hospital. They were ploughing through the wreckage and the bodies in their path, they were shooting, they were bombing. We were sure they were coming, they were going to enter the hospital, they were going to kill us. Those moments carried a dread that can't be described. We were living between life and death, we clung to hope while reality collapsed around us. The tanks advanced, and we were prepared for death. I was absolutely exhausted, worn out, but I fought against closing my eyes, I expected to see a tank gun barrel enter the room at any moment and fire. The tanks got louder, the sound of scraping rang in my ears. I imagined the bodies being mashed into the rubble beneath the tank treads. I dozed off briefly. It was one, maybe two in the morning when the sound of gunfire suddenly exploded. Bullets hit the ceiling and we screamed in terror. A woman next to us was shot. We moved quickly and gathered together in a huddle. The Israeli soldiers were entering the hospital courtyard and firing in all directions. They were ordering us to come out into the courtyard. A man standing next to us began repeating in a panicked voice, 'We are patients, women and children! We are patients, women and children!'

I pulled my mother's bed to the courtyard as the Israeli soldiers had ordered, and we found ourselves surrounded by bodies piled up on top of each other. Their huge dogs were circling us and barking, bullets were spraying in between our feet and over our heads, the tank barrels were pointing straight at us, zannanat rose and swooped down. I passed out, I was dying from fear. Amal woke me up, she was the girl who had stayed with me all the time in the hospital.

The Israeli soldiers surrounded us and said loudly: *Stay where you are, you are forbidden to move.* It was my first time seeing an Israeli face to face. I was born and lived under siege, and this was the first time I was actually seeing them. They yelled again: *Sit down, raise your hands and your heads!* They asked us to raise our heads, then they sent in their deadly flying machines to identify us by our irises. I was genuinely afraid that the quadcopter would blow off my head when they made it hover directly above me. They ordered the young men to stand on the right, one of them accidentally went the wrong way and they shot him instantly. I screamed. The young man bled out until he died. They stopped an old man – his father, perhaps – from going near him. After checking everyone's irises, they ordered one of the children with us to go and smash every surveillance camera. He did what they asked at gunpoint, he was just a little kid. Then they stormed the building. They went into all the wards. They began searching for people we didn't know. They took some of the patients and began beating them, their wounds split open from the beating. After that, they took all the remaining young men out to the courtyard, and there they stripped them naked. We could hear the sounds of torture. They shot two injured women who were lying in their beds, I saw them do it with my own eyes. One of the women died instantly.

After they had taken all the young men into the court-yard, it was the women's turn. They brought us out one after another, and reconfirmed our identity. The zannanat scrutinized us one by one. I was frightened they would harm us. They told us to squat with our heads down, and we stayed still in that position for two hours. Then there was the sound of a large explosion and we didn't know what had happened. We were looking at each other, making sure we were still alive. They took us back into the hospital building and began searching our bags. They took all the documents, and many other things. We stayed in the room overlooking the street. It was four o'clock in the morning when the Israelis left the Indonesian Hospital building, and we didn't know where they went. The following day, when we woke up, there was no sound of bombing and not a single Israeli soldier anywhere. We were in a different world. We couldn't understand this silence, then we discovered there was a ceasefire. When the hospital doors were opened, I saw daylight. By some fluke, we've survived, I told myself.

Outside the hospital, I saw for myself what I had never in my life imagined I would see. It will never be erased from my memory until I die. I saw corpses flung about and piled up on top of each other, human limbs scattered everywhere. Cars had been overturned and burned out, buildings and houses were destroyed – destruction was everywhere. The ground was sown with bodies, human limbs sprouted from the edge of the road, and in every corner, as far I could see, I saw people turning bodies over, looking for their children. My family were with them, looking for us among the martyrs. They found it a miracle that we had left the hospital alive. Am I sad? I don't know! What does sadness mean, in the face of everything I've said? What does it mean, in face of everything I've seen and can't say aloud? Everything becomes alike, and meaningless.

They took us to Kamal Adwan Hospital and we stayed there for three nights. We couldn't find beds there, so we slept on the floor. There were no doctors, no nurses, nothing. All of us, the wounded and the displaced, were on top of one another, it was a hospital in name only. I went out to see what happened to our house and my grandfather's house. I was still limping. I didn't find anything. My grandfather's house had vanished. It was non-existent, and our house was non-existent too, there was no building there at all, everything had been destroyed. My life and my childhood had vanished. The buildings had been razed to the ground. I couldn't recognize the place.

We survived a second massacre that took place in Kamal Adwan Hospital when the Israelis set fire to the tents of the displaced people. By chance, we weren't there at that moment. By a miracle, we survived more massacres on our way south. We fled from bombing to yet more bombing, and in the end we were split up. Each of us was in a different hospital, my mother was placed in a school for displaced people in al-Mawasy Khan Younis, her other leg was on the verge of amputation, and little by little she began to lose her hearing. Eventually we were able to gather once more in Rafah. We met in Rafah Camp, but that was another hell I won't speak about.

MUHAMMAD HAMDAN
65 years old
Khan Younis

I woke up at half past six on the morning of Saturday 7
October. I was surprised to find my daughters at my
house in Khan Younis; they'd come from every corner of Gaza. I didn't know, then, what was going on – I
learned about the events when I woke up. I live in a building of four floors, together with my siblings and their
children, where the whole family lived together. In the
shadow of war, the children all gathered at my house. We
couldn't believe what was happening. I was dumbstruck.
Who could imagine this? Back then, I said I will not leave
my house, and that's how everyone stayed with me for a
month and a half, despite the intensity of the bombing.

As the situation intensified, the children decided that
we should leave for Hamad, where the tower blocks are,
as we believed it would be away from the bombardment.
I used to work as a plumber, and I have a large family,
but I was responsible for everything – I would try and
manage all the household matters and care for them all.
I have two apartments that I allocated to my daughters,
and we all moved there. I am responsible for my family's
lives. I would gather my children and grandchildren at
night and ask them what they needed, and I would write
it all down so I could make sure they didn't want for anything, but the war escalated and in November, before
the ground operation, they began bombing the tower
blocks in Hamad. They destroyed the building façades,
the streets became ruins. We thought the place was safe,
but with the bombardment, we were displaced along with
the people. They only left a place when they had bombed
it. My house has been bombed before, and before that we

lost my daughter's husband, from the Abu Jalaba family. My son was hit the same way, and we buried him in those difficult days. My daughter lived with me in an apartment in Hamad. We were six families with children, including me and my wife. Everyone was looking to me, and I said to myself I must keep being strong in front of them. But as the bombing intensified on the area around the tower blocks, and things in Hamad got more dangerous, I eventually agreed with the family's decision to leave. My sister joined us, making us seven families with children. We didn't have anywhere else to go, everywhere was being bombed – where could I pitch a tent? We decided to move to my sister's house close to the Red Crescent, where a four-storey building housed four families. We all moved to a small apartment, there were about thirty-five of us. That was a hard decision to make, but we agreed to stay together. We would die together or survive together, and I couldn't leave them – my whole existence was to serve them and look after them. I didn't want to be displaced again, but fate decreed that I lose them all on 7 December.

I remember that before they died. I bought them a large quantity of food because there were so many children; also, the water was cut off and there was no electricity. On the day they died, I picked up my grand-daughter, who was two months old, and played with her. I asked everyone whether they needed anything to cook, and they replied that they needed water. I had to go out in the bombing to get the water. I chose five of my grand-sons, and we picked up containers and bottles. I waited until I couldn't hear planes any more, and I told the children we would go out quickly and come back, and out we went. The Red Crescent building was nearby, and I told the children, 'Let's go on a quick errand, we'll fetch water and go back.' We finished the first lot of water and went back for a second. The building was crammed full of people, they had gathered there thinking that this area would never be bombed. We were filling the water for the second time when a horrendous boom rang out. I felt something then, my heart told me that something terrible had happened, and I said, 'Allahumm 'awwid 'aleya.'* I had five boys with me, I couldn't leave them in the chaos of the bombing, people were running around and into each other like it was the Day of Hashr, the kids were screaming. The building they had bombed was just one street away from the Red Crescent building. I left the children with a friend and ran to the building, and while I was running, I saw the body of my son, Omar Muhammad Hamdan, and I saw his beautiful daughter who was barely two months old, and three other corpses, one of them was his wife. I stopped, in a daze. I was staring while they brought them out from under the rubble, their faces were lit up. I was seeing them for the last time without believing it.

In the first half hour, I completely collapsed, but I had to pull myself together and I joined the first responders as they brought out the corpses one after another, to confirm who was dead, who was wounded and who was alive. I had to account for every member of my family. The destruction was tremendous, and I lost hope. I told myself, 'Be strong, ya rajul. Alhamdulillah.' After that half hour was past, I felt as though my head was melting like liquid. Thirty members of my family alone had died. There were so many casualties I can no longer remember them all.

I stayed with the first responders, guiding them to places where people were stuck under the rubble and saying, 'So-and-so's still here, so-and-so's still there,

* A prayer said in hard times. Roughly translated, it means, 'May God compensate me', i.e. may God provide better times in compensation for the bad.

pull them out, look for them under the rubble.' I had left them preparing food while I brought water for them to drink, but they vanished. It took us three days to bring out the bodies, and we buried them after the afternoon prayer. My grandson was still alive, I found him fifteen days later in intensive care. His name is Muhammad Ali Ahmad Hamdan. He was recorded as 'name unknown' because his severe injuries had disfigured his features. He couldn't even see at first, and we found him by chance. I was looking for the corpse of my oldest son and they told us to search intensive care, as sometimes corpses and casualties were moved there without being identified. I had thought at the time that I would find my son, but I found my grandson, the only survivor from my family, the son of my son, who was identified later. His mother also died, so I stayed by his side – it was a miracle we had found him. I thanked the Lord I had found him. They told us his condition was hopeless and he gave no signs of life, but when he heard my voice, he started crying. I said, then, I would never leave him as long as I was alive. My son's friends stood by my side, they never abandoned me. I still remember that day, when they bombed the whole building. The iron melted, the stones mixed with earth. I felt some little comfort when I could pull out the bodies of my family with all their limbs intact, apart from my sister's young son who was torn to pieces, and I buried them with my own hands. Alhamdulillah, they were whole! In Gaza, it's important to us to know where our dead are buried, and that we can find their bodies. There are whole families which have disappeared from the civil register and no longer exist. I was relieved because I could bury them decently. I had been afraid for the bodies of my children and grandchildren – the Israelis were entering graveyards and taking bodies, so I had to ensure that my dead were safe. And so I moved all their corpses to the family graveyard.

They live here, in my head, they don't leave me for a moment. Sometimes I think I will kill myself, but I believe in God, and I am patient. I have lost my entire life at the end of my days – I am an old man, and my children have all gone in their youth. Now, I am with my grandson, the only survivor from my family, who is suffering from a fractured skull. I care for him, I hope that he lives to know what happened to his family. His small body is full of shrapnel, his feet are broken; his whole body is filled with platinum. He still needs operations. I want to care for him and give him a chance at life. I remember the day of the explosion, when they brought out my family, corpse after corpse, I couldn't see straight. The neighbours could see me, but I couldn't make them out. I spent that night sitting next to the bodies before they were buried. Since that day, every day, I go out into the street and walk aimlessly. I can't see, I can't sleep, even sleeping pills don't work on me.

Please, remember their names, please remember them and don't forget, remember some of them at least.

My wife: Jamila Mahmoud Hamdan

My daughter: Duaa Hamdan

Wafaa and her children: Ismail, Ala and Ghana

Safaa Hamdan and her two daughters: Maryam and Layal Abu Jalaba

My sister Fadwa Muhammad Hamdan and her daughter, Amani Abu Jalaba, and her son Ahmed Abu Jalaba

My son Mahmoud Hamdan

My son Omar Hamdan and his wife, Ala Zarqout.

HAJIR ABU SAMAAN
30 years old
Gaza City

On the morning of 7 October, I was awake and getting my kids ready for school: 11-year-old Salwa, 10-year-old Sara, and Nasser, who is 6. The sound of rockets took us by surprise.

In Gaza, we are basically living in a prison, constantly subject to wars and bombardment. The first bombing lasted for three weeks, and we didn't leave the house. We used to think they would never bomb us, as we are civilians and the Israelis know that, but they bombed everyone. The building we live in consists of three floors, and it belongs to my husband's family. There were also other relatives who were displaced and came to us. At the time, there were forty people in it, when the fire belt started. Dozens of missiles falling all at once, the sound of the explosions was horrific, as if the ground was splitting open. One wave lasted perhaps for four hours, with missiles falling dozens at a time without a break. We were scared to death, or rather we expected to die at any moment, and we constantly recited the two shahadas. The result is well-known – the massacre of al-Jalaa* where 200 people died. It was close to us, we could hear the explosions. The Baptist [Hospital] massacre was just the same. We were surrounded by massacres, waiting our turn. I would gather the building's children, trying to lighten the horror for them. I would recite the Qur'an to them, we would draw and colour together. We were painting in the middle of death and destruction. My son Nasser would spend the night under the sofa. He would refuse to come out, stuffing himself underneath it, his

* See the testimony of Firas Sheikh Radwan.

head between his hands, his tense body constantly trembling. Sometimes he would fold up as if he was a circle that wanted to disappear. Seeing him like that gave me a mixture of fear and pity. I would say to him, 'Come here and sit in my lap, you're safe with me,' and he would hurry over to me and curl up in my arms, burying his head in my chest. Those were difficult days, and as the bombing increased, so did the children's fear and screams. Just the sound of the zannanat was frightening but we were also scared that they might come inside, as they had entered other houses. It began to be a habit that I slept with my children in one room, usually in the living room, thinking we were safer together – Nasser in my lap, Salwa and Sara curled up on top of me – and my husband would sleep in another room. That was how we were on the night they bombed our building. They hit us with two missiles. Our building had three storeys and I lived on the first floor. The windows went flying, the doors blew off, the two floors above us collapsed. The ceiling of the living room, where we were sleeping, collapsed as well. It fell on us, bringing with it the bodies of six of my husband's relatives. They had been asleep in the living room just above us, they told me later.

The bombing happened on the night of 2 November. I woke up as though from a deep sleep to find myself in hospital with one leg. My husband told me that my leg had been severed immediately by the bomb, and they had buried it with the bodies and limbs of those who had been killed in the attack. The bodies of our relatives were simply limbs, broken into pieces. The body parts had been mixed up together, mashed into the wreckage, scattered everywhere. They didn't know what part belonged to which person. They found a child's head on the roof of a neighbouring building. Anyone who wasn't killed was

90

wounded.

My husband said that the strike penetrated the upper two floors, causing a crack in the living room ceiling that collapsed and severed my leg. I had chosen the living room to sleep in, thinking it was safe. My husband said that straight after the bombing he saw our son Nasser's head in among the debris and thought he was dead. Then he realized that Nasser was injured, with deep wounds in his head, his stomach and his leg. My husband picked him up and ran, looking for a car. Everyone in the neighbourhood had their own wounded they were occupied with, but that didn't stop them from helping each other. A neighbour took my son in their car and my husband came back to look for me. I was buried underneath the debris, wounds everywhere in my body, covered in blood, my leg cut off. He thought I was dead, but my daughter told him she had heard me moan. Salwa suffered from burns, but she had stayed conscious during and after the bombing – she saw everything. As for Sara, the missile consumed her flesh and gave her disfiguring wounds all over her body.

At first they thought Nasser was dead, so as soon as our neighbours brought him to the hospital, they put him next to the bodies of children who had passed in the massacres. The nurses put him with the unknown children as they didn't know his name or whose son he was. The numbers of people were immense, things were chaotic. Then, when my husband arrived, he couldn't find Nasser. The congestion was suffocating, people were wandering everywhere, bodies were lying on the ground and everyone was looking for the bodies of their families and relatives. My husband couldn't find Nasser's body. My son was lost! They thought he was dead so they'd put him with the other children's bodies, but when the time came to bury them, they discovered Nasser was alive and rushed him to surgery. They performed an operation on his head, they removed his spleen, and they amputated his foot below the heel. After he woke up from his operation, he heard them saying he was a lost child without a name. He told them he wasn't lost, he had a name and a family. He began yelling, 'I am not lost, I have a family, my name is Nasser Abu Samaan.' No one turned to him. That day was like the Day of Hashr: the killed, the injured, people looking for their relatives among the corpses and the lists of the injured, chaos, screaming and howling everywhere. How could anyone hear anything? No one heard him, and Nasser kept screaming, 'I am not lost, I have a family, I am Nasser Abu Samaan.' My husband kept looking for our son among the martyrs, in every hospital ward, until he eventually found him two days later. All that time, I was lying on my hospital bed like a corpse, I couldn't move any part of my body, not even my head. I could only see the ceiling. I didn't know yet that my leg had been cut off. Actually, I don't remember now when I learned I had lost it. Everything happened so quickly and strangely, in a hospital where doctors kept working night and day, and all the wounded had serious injuries and needed endless surgeries.

When my husband came and told me he had found Nasser, I thanked God. After that, they brought him to me. I noticed that he relaxed when he saw me. He smiled, I smiled. He couldn't run towards me and I couldn't run towards him. In fact neither of us could hug the other. We made do with looking at each other and smiling.

A week later, the hospital was under siege. My husband considered moving us to the Baptist Hospital, which was resuming work after the massacre. How would I be transferred? I couldn't move at all, not even my fingers. My entire body was in pain – breathing was painful, the agony was indescribable and I only had one leg. I told him, 'If I am moved, I will die.' He tried in vain to convince me. All I could think of was my children, I wanted them to survive and to live. I convinced him to take the children to the Baptist Hospital. As for me, I would remain at al-Shifa and my brother would care for me. A week after I was admitted to al-Shifa Hospital, it was under siege. Then the Israelis stormed it. They killed many people. My brother kept coming and going, telling me what he saw. They fired on everyone, bodies were spread everywhere, left lying on the ground where dogs and cats ate them. On our beds inside the wards, we heard the horrifying stories of what was happening outside and believed that we should expect the same fate. The doctors and nurses never abandoned us, they were utterly dedicated. They told us, 'We have taken the medical oath, we are not leaving our injured patients, we will remain with you, we live together or we die together.' There were wounds across every inch of my body, some of them long and deep. Because my dressings were changed, so that the wounds wouldn't get infected and maggots wouldn't eat me, I am still alive – but the problem was that there were no painkillers or tranquillisers, and changing the dressings was complete agony. I would scream at the nurse to kill me, I couldn't bear the pain, I didn't want to live. The nurse, along with other nurses and doctors, dealt with me calmly and compassionately, asking me to be patient, to keep enduring. I never stopped crying, truly, I wasn't able to stop. It felt as though knives were slicing my flesh, I was dying a thousand times over and coming back to life. Every second was a death and a return to life, all at the same time.

We suffered a lot from the lack of water and food. We

drank salt water from the pipes, and after a while we couldn't even manage to get that, so some of the young men began to risk their lives to go out and bring us back a little water. We were hungry, everyone was starving, I heard the children crying from hunger. And throughout all this, we were being bombed and the Israeli soldiers might have stormed our rooms at any moment. I was suffering, and I could hear, but I was powerless to move or do anything. They bombed the hospital's maternity building and we heard awful stories about what was happening there. I can't relate everything I heard, I just can't. They bombed the neonatal ward, which held somewhere between twenty and thirty premature babies, I can't remember the exact number. Some of them died, one after another, then they brought out the rest, so I heard. Who brought them out? Where did they take them? Did they know their names and their families? What has happened to those babies? What has happened to their mothers? I was on my bed, hearing these stories, and I thought about the mothers, and I was in so much pain. The bombing was relentless, phone reception was cut off, the wounded and the corpses were everywhere, I had no way of knowing if my husband and children were all right or what was happening to them. My brother stayed with me. He cared for me and risked himself to bring some water and tinned food, which put me in constant fear for him. We had a few dates, I ate perhaps one or two dates per day.

Four days before the end of the siege, an order came for everyone, all the doctors, nurses and patients, to leave the hospital. Only those who were in a critical state or bedbound would remain. As for everyone who could move, even if it was on crutches or in a wheelchair, they had to leave through the safe corridor. That's what they called it! A safe corridor! It was a street – I've forgotten its name now – I swear to God, everyone went out and walked along it. I stayed behind because of my condition, along with others with critical injuries, and five doctors and four nurses stayed with us. We all went down to the basement level. I saw injured people left lying there, their families had left them and gone. I remember a man whose son had left him alone. His wounds had rotted until maggots started coming out of them. The man was silent and never said a word. In those days, my brother was the one to change my dressings, he had learned from watching the nurses.

We anticipated bombardment, we were waiting for it – we expected death every moment. We never imagined they would storm the building. But they did. This happened four days after the evacuation. They entered the hospital, they took the doctors and stripped off their clothes, they beat the nurses, they arrested or killed the young men and this made me terrified for my brother. Then they called out over the loudspeaker that they wanted to search the patients, so they gathered us together, and the inspecting soldiers came over bristling with weapons. They stripped all the men naked and they searched us.

On the evening of the ceasefire, the Israelis threw us out of the hospital. Everything that happened until that point was on one hand, and everything that happened afterwards was on the other. They piled us up in a single ambulance, me and four other injured people, two children and two adults. The ambulance kept jolting us the whole way, my body was directly touching the metal, and my wounds were uncovered. With every shake, the pain butchered me. The convoy was made up of seventeen ambulances and we waited for nine hours at the Netzarim checkpoint until it was our ambulance's turn to be inspected. I could hear my groaning getting weaker and weaker, until I thought I was dead. The Israelis mistakenly believed that the wounded man next to me was wanted, so they put a gun to his head. I closed my eyes at that, believing they would shoot him. On the other side of me was a woman embracing her injured daughter. The girl had been hit in the head; she had had an operation but it hadn't succeeded in stabilizing her head, which kept twitching and jerking. A soldier yelled at the mother to keep her daughter's head still. The mother told him it was one of the complications of her injury. The Israelis wanted to scan the girl's eye. Several soldiers came and they held the girl still and did the scan. I couldn't understand what has happening, soldiers gathering to hold a 7-year-old girl's head still to take a picture of her eye. Was this girl a threat to the world? My God! Nine hours we waited at the Netzarim checkpoint, under the eyes of the UN and the Red Crescent. The Israelis arrested the paramedics, the nurses and the five doctors. They arrested a female first responder from the Red Crescent. They arrested Dr Muhammad Abu Salmiya, but by some miracle my brother escaped arrest. The UN didn't do a thing – it all happened in front of their employees' eyes.

The hours of inspection and waiting at Netzarim checkpoint passed like a century. The inspection finished and the ambulances went on their way. We were travelling under bombardment, and along the way, human body parts and rotting corpses were lying as far as the eye could see. They took me to a school, because the hospital was full with patients and displaced people. The Indonesian Hospital was under siege, and the other hospitals weren't equipped to accept more. They put me on a metal bed without a mattress, my body was directly on the iron. I was screaming in pain the whole time, and so was the girl, the same one with the open head who couldn't stop jerking. She screamed horrifyingly. On the following day, they said they had prepared field hospitals for us, in a tent furnished with some medical supplies. My aunt did her best to get me transferred to one of these tents in an ambulance, and meanwhile they changed my dressings in the European Hospital. During that ceasefire, I learned what had happened to my mother, father and siblings over the previous two months. They had been displaced time and time again, from Hayy al-Daraj to al-Jalaa, then to al-Zeitoun, and after that to al-Shuja'iyya. I was lying on my bed while they were suffering, forced from place to place with bombs chasing them at every turn. Then I learned that one of my brothers was martyred. His name was Ibrahim. He was bringing drinking water to people when a drone targeted him. My husband and children were still in the Baptist Hospital. We were split up, separated from each other and sent in every direction. I still haven't seen my family and my children.

There are so many images that never leave my mind.

Flies covering us while we were in the hospital.

Blood on the floor tiles.

The cats who would gnaw on corpses then come inside with red faces. Looking at them, we knew it was human blood.

The bodies lining the roads on our way to Netzarim, and then away from Netzarim.

The girl opposite me in the field hospital, bleeding to death. Her leg was severed and there was no one with us. She kept bleeding and bleeding, and little by little she lost consciousness until she died.

I remember a girl from the al-Khouly family, 5 years old. When the missile fell on their building, everyone was killed – her father, her mother, uncles and aunts on both sides. She survived because the blast sent her flying, along with two of her sisters. One of her sisters was burned all over her body, I don't know if the other died or survived. The girl I'm telling you about lost her legs. She was with me in al-Shifa Hospital, she was called Iman al-Khouly. I remember another orphan girl called Hala Duhshan, and a third called Dareen al-Biyaa. Seventy members of her family were killed – everyone knows their story. So many names in my head, the names of children whose entire families have vanished, the whole family of uncles and aunts and relatives. I also remember images of the hunger. My family in Hayy al-Daraj used to mix animal feed with flour. Yes! They ate animal feed. People were murdered on account of flour, the price of one bag reached a thousand dollars. They would get into fights when they were collecting aid, or while they were waiting for a bag of flour. Some of them died for it.

And then there are all the things that cannot be spoken.

MUHAMMAD YASIR ABU SAEED
18 years old
Al-Bureij Camp

On 7 October I was getting ready to go to school, and while I was washing my face I saw the rockets falling. We haven't been to school since that day. I was injured at the beginning of the war, on 26 October. I live with my family: my father, Yasir Muhammad Abu Saeed, my mother, Rana Abu Zayed, and my brother who was born during the war. All together, we were five boys and two girls. We used to live like any other family in the shadow of war, we tried to adapt our daily lives. We have grown up through wars. My family worked in the chicken farms. We would leave for work at six in the morning and come back at four in the afternoon, despite the non-stop bombing. When school stopped because of the war, I worked in the farms with my family. We were normal civilians. We didn't expect the war to continue with such intensity, we thought it wouldn't harm us. We carried on with our daily lives until 26 October.

That day, we woke up as usual and headed east to work in the chicken farms. While we were working, the bombing started all around us. I went back home in a car with a group, there were twelve of us in a pickup truck, and the bombs followed us. We were heading from east to west Gaza and the back section of the truck was open. Shrapnel began flying around us from every direction. They fired six missiles at us. The sixth fell on the truck without exploding, but shrapnel from another one hit us. My cousin lost his lower leg, I was hit in the leg, another cousin lost his heel. My brother was sent flying by the explosion and slammed into a tree. We all went flying from the force of the missiles.

There were no first responders that early morning, and no one around to help us. I stayed on the ground until a man came past in a car and took us to al-Aqsa Hospital where they put us in the Reception Department. I wasn't fully conscious, I was hallucinating. I saw the missile, then total blackness overwhelmed me. I didn't hear the sound of the explosion until after I was hit. I tried to pull the shrapnel out of my leg. I drifted in and out of consciousness. The shrapnel consumed the flesh of my leg. There was nothing left of it.

When we got to the hospital, the nurses picked me up. It felt like I was in a dark place. Triangular shapes appeared in front of me, the world was spinning me round, blackness enveloped me completely. I thought I was in a grave. I felt that I was dead and I was speaking to people but no one could hear me. I was sure I was dead. I could see blue triangles and black circles, I was screaming and crying out, but it was no use. My voice wasn't reaching anyone even though my lips were moving. When I woke up, I saw my leg was strapped to a piece of metal and I found myself on a wooden bed. The pain in my back was horrendous. There was no mattress on the bed, just wood, and I was yelling and hallucinating from the pain. I realized that the bombing was still going on.

They tied my leg to the bed, it was bleeding. My cousin and brother were nearby. Even though I was blacking out and not fully conscious, I saw a doctor putting a solution on me, and I could see blood everywhere – red flooded my vision. They did an operation on my leg: the bone was completely shattered so they put in platinum plates to support it. I spent three months in hospital, and during that time I saw suffering and torment. The sound of explosions never left me, and the colour of blood was constantly fixed in front of my eyes. We were in a large room in the hospital, I don't know if it was an actual room or an open space like a prison barracks. People surrounded me, some on the ground, others on beds. I couldn't move, the corridors were crammed with displaced people, all piled on top of one another.

In the first month things were OK, but after that we lost everything. No medical equipment, no food, not even water. I was in a critical state – my body was eaten away and torn up, I needed strong painkillers to ease the pain while my dressings were changed. Half of my flesh was shredded, and all my body was filled with craters. I heard non-stop gunfire and bombing, and I heard them saying we had to evacuate al-Aqsa Hospital. That was on 15 February. There was nowhere else for us to go, so I stayed another day. On the third day, the hospital began emptying. I called my father and told him I had to leave. My father was in al-Zawayda, he came and took me. I was horrified at the thought of having my legs amputated. The doctors decided to amputate them both, because they were just bones with no flesh. I absolutely refused, I insisted many times, over and over, that I preferred death over having my legs amputated, and I decided to discharge myself from treatment so I wouldn't lose them.

I went to my grandmother's house with my father. I used to go out at night in a wheelchair, sometimes examining the streets, seeing how people were. But I stopped doing that after I saw people gathering up body parts – bodies stuffed inside blankets, bodies cut up like hunks of meat. That's when I decided to stay in bed so I wouldn't see any more horrors like that. In the last stage of my hospital stay, I used to ask for help moving my bed so I could see what was happening around me. That was madness. Once, in the first month, I was sitting on my wheelchair in the biting cold, under a tree, when I heard shouting and a pickup truck arrived. They were moving victims from a massacre in Deir al-Balah. I saw heads and guts, scraps of bodies put in plastic bags like cuts of meat. Altogether, it made me prefer not to move from my bed or to leave the hospital. I said that death was now the better option, so I waited for it, in the bombing around the hospital. My mother's family lost more than thirty members in October, in Deir al-Balah. There are so many stories and countless massacres, I can't find the words any more to describe what I've seen. Limbs, less-than-half-bodies. People were simply dying. One of them died next to me, all alone. He stank and his body was rotting away while he was still alive. He died alone.

AMAL ADHAM
24 years old
Beit Lahia

I have been married since I was 16, my husband is from Beit al-Ghaban and we live close to my family home. On 7 October, because our house is close to the border with the Israelis, we decided to leave at once when we felt a ground assault was on its way. We sheltered in one of the schools, we became displaced. Danger clung to us, but even so we stayed put, returning occasionally to our house. One of these times, my brother was in the house when it was bombed, and when my mother went to visit him in hospital, she was bombed on the way there. She disappeared for an entire day, and all that time we didn't know her whereabouts or her fate. The missile struck her while she was in the al-Saftawy region, and we lost all trace of her. Where did she vanish to? She was in the hospital, but no one recognized her because her face had been so disfigured. When we found her in the hospital the following day, her face wasn't my mother's. It was covered in a bandage, her body was full of deep wounds and there were platinum plates in both her legs. I only recognized her by her voice. I was in a state of deep shock, and asked myself, 'Is this really my mother?' When she screamed, 'Amal, don't leave me!' then I knew it was her. I spent a month at her side in the Indonesian Hospital, and I saw things there I can't put into words. I saw what happened with my own eyes, and I can't believe I am still alive. Every day I ask myself, am I really alive or am I in a nightmare?

We entered mid-October 2023 and I couldn't understand the things I was seeing on a daily basis. People without limbs, without hands, without eyes, decapitated corpses. Noises, the colours of blood, disgusting smells filled the place, human bodies that no longer seemed human. Children like piled-up chops of meat. I never saw a whole body, I couldn't remember what a whole body was like, I couldn't. The smells were always there, the smell of rot coming from corpses and living bodies. There was no water, food or medicine. I saw people decomposing right in front me, both the dead and the living. Maggots burst out of living bodies, and there was nothing the doctors could do about it. So I volunteered as a nurse, and my friend volunteered with me. We put on plastic gloves and set to work. Despite our lack of skills, we tried to do what we could. All the while, the Israeli planes kept bombing the hospital. They hit the solar panels that generated electricity. Tanks surrounded the place. I wouldn't have believed what was happening if I hadn't seen it for myself. No electricity, no water, nothing. That was how the Israelis laid siege to the Indonesian Hospital. In intensive care, the patients were on the verge of death. Then the Israelis bombed the third floor, where the paediatric ward was. I ran there, I saw the bodies. They had bombed a hospital full of children. I left the bombed floor and went back to my mother. I took her to a corridor away from the bombs and told myself, 'I will die by her side.' I slept on the floor next to her, and the bombing carried on without a break. We decided not to surrender. We cleaned the place as best we could after the bombardment and told ourselves, 'We will die, but until then we will do what we can.' I remember that day, it was a Thursday, the hardest day of my life, as we went down the basement, cleaned it up and sheltered there. Suddenly they blew open the door and rushed in on us. There were lots of children, old people, wounded and amputees with us. I saw a woman suddenly start bleeding from her eye, like a fountain. We all froze, watching in a daze. I told her, 'Your eye's bleeding!' She just kept standing stock still, like a stone. She didn't move. She had been hit in the eye by a piece of shrapnel when they blew open the door. She didn't scream in fear, perhaps she was so afraid she didn't even feel any pain. After that, they gathered us in the hospital courtyard, and approached us with their dogs and guns. I saw an old woman in her eighties, injured and sitting on the ground there. They killed her straight away, just by the way they entered. She didn't make a sound, she didn't even groan. After that they shot twice at a young man they wanted dead. There were about 180 of us. They entered with tanks and drones, and we were nailed to the spot. We raised our hands in surrender.

We knelt down and raised our hands while they stripped the clothes off every man over 20, they made us girls stand to the side. They began shouting at us, ordering us to halt. One of the nurses, her name is Asma, they searched her and she told them, 'I'm just a nurse,' but they didn't believe her. After that they scanned everyone's irises. We were surrounded by snipers with guns trained on us, we began shaking from cold and fear. The young men were shaking too, after they made them stand half-naked in just their underwear. They inspected us women one by one. That was a dark day in every sense of the word. I said goodbye to my mother, saying, 'Forgive me, Ummi, I might not come back.' My mother was bedbound, she couldn't move, so we moved her in her bed.

I don't understand how I lived and why I stayed alive. We were all praying, waiting to die. We knew we were going to die. They were beating the injured on their wounds and their amputated stumps, mocking them, saying they weren't really sick. I know most of those people, all of them were disabled and amputees. I saw them myself. What I can't forget most of all is how they went into the room for washing the dead, they stormed in with tanks, they ran over the bodies with tanks, dead bodies being crushed all over again. I saw this with my own eyes.

After they withdrew, we stayed in the corridor. The cold was bitter and we were frightened. The Red Cross came later on to evacuate people from the hospital. After they left, we saw a large number of dead, disfigured in ways I can't describe. Until that moment, we hadn't fully realized that what had happened was a massacre. We were in the heart of it.

I can't forget their terrifying voices, their dogs. They were searching everywhere, asking about Hamas and the hostages. We were just wounded people, most of us elderly, women and children, most of us were amputees because of the bombing. I remember that we didn't even dare open the windows. They would snipe us if we went near them, their drones would kill us. The bombing, which never stopped, drove us insane. Once, my friend and I tried to get some things from the upper floor. As soon as they saw us, they shot at us, so we were forced to throw ourselves on the ground and leave everything behind. We couldn't move even within the hospital, we were like mice in a trap. I also remember when the water disappeared from the bathrooms, there wasn't a single drop of water. That was a very difficult situation for us women.

I am afraid of the sight of blood, I used to black out. But suddenly, I felt strong, and responsible for treating the injured. Imagine it, I was mixing hydrogen peroxide with the saline solution for cleaning wounds. That chemical was dangerous, if I made a mistake in measuring out the quantity, it could have been lethal. I tried it first on my mother's leg, then I used it to clean the wounds of others. I don't know how I did it, I don't remember many of the details, but I did what I could. In intensive care, there were two people suffering from severe burns. They asked for a drink of water and I knew they were dying. I began to cry when I saw maggots coming out of their bodies. They were just lumps of flesh being eaten up in front of me, and I couldn't do anything apart from give them water to drink. I couldn't believe I was still alive after this experience, I stayed in a state of shock. I went to my mother, I hugged her and shouted, 'I'm alive!' My mother replied, 'You're alive!' I looked around, there were bodies scattered everywhere. My mother and I looked into each other's eyes in disbelief.

They had smashed all the hospital's instruments and equipment, they trampled the medicines with tanks so they couldn't be used. They arrested nurses and patients, even the amputees.

We left at six in the morning on Friday, the day of the ceasefire, and we headed south. When we left the hospital gate, I saw someone come to identify the body of one of his relatives, only to find that the dogs had eaten his face. The bodies crushed by the tanks were so deformed that it was impossible to identify them. People were walking around numbly, looking at us and in total disbelief that we were alive. Meanwhile, others were searching among the limbs. I remember that when the Israelis stormed the hospital and claimed they were coming to protect us, after they killed the wounded old woman, a little boy said to them, 'Does that mean you'll bring some food?' Hunger was on the point of killing us. Like that boy, we were in shock. When we arrived at Salah al-Din checkpoint, they stopped us and tortured us during the inspection, they tortured the injured patients as well. I was confused, my head was twitching from trauma. They began yelling into microphones, we were all on the point of collapse, the sick and the dismembered. They asked everyone to get off, but how could we? None of them could move! Of the fifty people on the bus, I was able to get off, and so was one other woman, as for the rest, they were amputees. They asked: *No one else?* I was frozen with terror, they could see the amputees right there. They took the girl who was next to me, then one of the soldiers said to me, *You, go back.* I was frozen, I felt as though I couldn't move. I said, 'I can't walk.' So they dragged me. We stayed there for an hour as they searched us, while I was frozen rigid next to my mother. After that hell was over, we went to Nasser Hospital.

They arrested my father on 7 October, he was just a labourer and he stayed in their custody for two months – we didn't know anything about him. When he came out of prison, his body kept shaking from the brutal torture he had faced. He told us how they would tie their hands and legs and make them sleep on sharp gravel. When my father came out, he was 50 years old, his body completely broken down. They were thrown out naked and hand-cuffed, without food or drink. My father escaped death in detention, but afterwards a drone shot him in the neck and killed him.

IBRAHIM QUDAIH
21 years old
Khan Younis

Before the war, I was studying nursing at al-Azhar University and I was in my second year. All studies stopped at the beginning of the war on 7 October, which has destroyed all the universities in the Gaza Strip and deprived thousands of students of their right to education. Before the war, I spent the summer holiday with my mother's family in Morocco and returned to Gaza on 12 September at night, having survived the Morocco earthquake while I was in the airport. I had a university exam, and afterwards I sat and chatted with my friends before term started. But on 7 October, Saturday, at half past six in the morning, the war began.

I'm from Abasan al-Kabira, a town two kilometres from the border of the Strip. It wasn't bombed at first, although I was fully aware the bombing would reach us eventually. On 8 October, the whole Gaza Strip witnessed fire belts and incessant bombardment, and alongside that the Israeli forces dropped leaflets demanding that we leave. These leaflets were pretexts, false warnings, nothing more; they were dropped on us along with the bombs. They demanded we move to safe 'humanitarian areas' but this was untrue as well, because all of Gaza was under fire. Missiles began falling around our house, the pitch of bombing increased as time went on, and many of my neighbours decided to flee, but I clung on in my house, believing in the saying, 'Man kharaja min darihi qalla miqdarihi.'* On 9 October, the bombing continued and we stayed, waiting to die without leaving our house, until

---

* Literally, 'whoever leaves his home reduces his value,' the implication being that leaving home diminishes a person.

10 October came, and the forces distributed new leaflets warning: *Leave or die*. They even used warning missiles to pressure us, so I was forced out with my family and we headed to Khan Younis to the house of a family friend. I drove my car through the middle of bombardment with missiles falling around, above, in front and behind, until we reached Khan Younis and my friend's house in Sheikh Nasser. The road was full of dangers, and all the way there I had the feeling that death was right around the corner.

With safe places so few, my friend's house was crammed full of displaced people: women on the first floor and young men on the second. I didn't take anything with me apart from two changes of clothes and some official documents, my education certificates and my passport. It felt like being born all over again, on 10 October.

That night, I decided to volunteer as a nurse in Nasser Hospital, hoping to be able to help people. I went to them and told them I was a second-year nursing student, and I wanted to volunteer. I volunteered from 10 to 17 October, and during that time I saw horrors in the hospital I don't know how to describe. I saw a women searching like a madwoman for her martyred children and screaming in the hospital precincts, 'Where are my children?' The whites of her eyes had turned red from weeping. I saw a child sliced in two, bodies without heads, guts sprayed everywhere, human pieces here and there. I'm 20 years old, I didn't imagine myself capable of enduring such things, but Gaza's children grow up fast. We've known war since infancy and the siege is part of our lives, we've grown up under it, and we're used to bombardment, but this wasn't war – this was something that surpassed all our experiences.

Despite the horror and the atrocities, I felt my duty was to remain with these people, so I stayed in the hospital. I worked in the middle of dead bodies, injured people and people with missing limbs. There was a boy of 10 who insisted on volunteering with us and gathering limbs, and he thrust himself in among us saying that he wouldn't leave until they accepted him being there. No one expected to see a child collecting pieces of other children. I saw so much, so much, and those scenes haunt me even now.

On 17 October, I finished a long shift at the hospital – twenty-four continuous hours under violent and constant bombardment. Food and drink were far from our minds, there was no time even to think of being hungry. The bombing didn't reach the hospital at the beginning of the war, but afterwards it extended over everything. After work, I passed a restaurant close to my friend's house and suddenly remembered it had been more than a day since I had last eaten. I wasn't the only one who was hungry – the entire medical team was in the same situation. I picked up a meal and hurried to my friend's house. Using a bottle of water, I cleaned myself hurriedly, as we usually did – you couldn't call it a proper wash – to try and avoid the risk of dying naked in a bombing. Even though I was starving, there was a choking pressure on my chest that stopped me from eating. I sat down suddenly, breathing deeply, trying to overcome the feeling of suffocation. It was like a terrible premonition was filling my soul. I sent messages to my friends and family – perhaps I was saying goodbye to them without realizing. It was almost two-thirty in the afternoon when a huge missile fell, something like an explosive barrel weighing a thousand kilograms, and it exploded 150 metres away, targeting a building opposite us. The explosion was so destructive that three of my limbs were severed in a single moment. It blasted me 200 metres through the air, and I found myself lying in an empty spot far away from people. The strike had made my vision blurry and confused, but my sense of hearing was still strong. I stayed there for about half an hour, shouting and calling for help, but there was no reply. After a while, I lost hope and began to give up, repeating the shahada, trying to calm myself by reciting the Qur'an. Minutes passed and I heard the sound of footsteps getting closer. It seemed as though someone was looking through the rubble for survivors. I screamed for help, 'Over here, I'm alive!' A voice came and it seemed to belong to a young boy, perhaps 15 years old, he called shakily, 'A martyr, a martyr!' I replied weakly, 'No, I'm injured, I'm still alive.' The boy came closer and there were two men with him who picked up my body, but I was too heavy for them and they fell over. There, I saw clearly that I was missing limbs, and when I asked the men if it was true, one of them replied, 'Yes, but remember to say Alhamdulillah.'

I was naked, still on the ground without anything covering me after the explosion tore through the bathroom and ripped me up, so I told the man who picked me up, 'Please, cover me up.' They covered me with a piece of cardboard and picked me up again, until we reached the ambulance where they put me inside with other corpses, some of them missing limbs and piled up next to me. The paramedic thought I was a martyr, but when he saw I was still breathing he asked me my name and my family. To his astonishment, I was able to reply clearly, despite the raging pain, my disfigured face and torn-up body

We arrived at Nasser Hospital, the hospital where I had previously volunteered, and when the first responder announced our arrival, I fell into a coma and a long period of darkness began. The coma lasted until the beginning of November, with short periods in between when I would wake up for a few seconds, then lose consciousness again. I could hear my surroundings but I couldn't see clearly, as though everything was covered in fog. The voices of the doctors and my family reached me but I was unable to respond, until one day my mother's voice came to me, saying with pure tenderness, 'Ibrahim, I'm here with you.' I woke up for a few seconds and called her, 'Mama, you came?' Then I went back into the coma. The following morning, I regained consciousness fully and began the journey of torment and treatment. Successive surgeries, relentless agony and dreadful hardship were waiting for me at every step.

My severed limbs were left behind at the site of the explosion – both feet, a hand and some fingers of the other hand. I learned later that my cousin visited the bombsite, found three of my body parts and then buried them, but I don't know where. It seems impossible that I ever will know – after the army of occupation destroyed the hospitals, it headed to the graveyards and dug them up and took the bodies. They destroyed any hope I had of visiting the buried half of my body. But perhaps someday, when I go back to Gaza, I will be able to search for that half.

Despite being a nurse, I faced indescribable horror. I have been inundated with nightmares since the first day of the war. I wake up to see atrocities, and I doze off only to meet with nightmares, a cycle that never ends. This isn't a war, it's genocide. I can't think of another description of what I have witnessed. I've had more than sixty surgeries. Some days, I underwent three in succession. My body has become a lump of scars and holes, my right hand was on the verge of being amputated, but the doctors saved it even though some fingers ended up being amputated. Two fingers are left, with support from a platinum plate. I can't believe I am still alive.

In the hospital, they began calling me al-Shahid al-Hayy, the Living Martyr. My body has become a mixture of wounds and shrapnel, but nevertheless, it is still breathing. I've undergone long operations, one lasted twelve full hours. On the forty-second day after I was injured, I heard one of them suggest turning off my machine because 'there's no hope of his survival'. I heard them saying, 'Take him to the mortuary fridge,' and discussing how the equipment was needed to save another patient whose chances might be better. I realized that I was on the brink of dying, so I summoned up my voice and managed to say, 'I'm alive!' I woke up for a few minutes and said in a weak voice, 'I'm great, I'm alive.' I kept repeating that for a couple of minutes, until I felt I had proved to them that I was alive. Then I blacked out, but from that moment some of my organs started working again.

Before my injury, I volunteered at Nasser Hospital where hundreds of wounded and displaced people passed every day, alongside hundreds of dead bodies. I moved through crowds drenched with blood and agony, helping however I could, but I never imagined I would one day form part of that suffering. I've been through gruelling times and horrendous pain to come back and be what I am now. I still can't believe I am alive.

My mother's presence at my side throughout the journey has given me the drive to keep going, to persevere in the face of this catastrophe. Before 7 October, I was strong and sporty, in excellent health, top of my class at university, I was living with my family and I loved life in Gaza. I still have dreams for the future, though. Even if I have lost half my body, my mind and soul are here, both unchanged. Now I aspire to write stories, to carry on with my studies and to return one day to the Gaza I love.

JIHAN BAKRY
30 years old
Khan Younis

I studied Arabic literature in Gaza, I am the mother of two children. Two days before 7 October, I was in hospital because of a severe pain in my abdomen. They discovered I had severe appendicitis so my husband took me to hospital, they performed surgery on me and I stayed to complete my treatment.

When the bombing started I was afraid for my children, so I didn't wait to finish the treatment and left the hospital. I took them from my family's house and brought them home with me. I stayed there for the first week of the war, never leaving the house, despite the intensity of the bombing and the pain I was suffering. We were living in Ma'an, in Khan Younis. Then the situation got worse, my husband couldn't bear the children's terror, his heart was breaking for them, I could see it in his eyes. He said he would stay and protect the house, and when he asked me to return to my family's house with them, I agreed at once. The children were terrified, they were frightened of the destruction, the strikes which surrounded us, and the buildings falling down all around.

On 12 October, I heard that the Israelis had bombed with a fire belt around our house. I was so frightened for my husband, there was no way of contacting him. That night, I tried to find news of him without success, then I learned he had been injured. I didn't know what was happening, the phones and electricity were cut off. At first, they said he was wounded, then they said he was getting worse, and before long they told me that my husband was killed in the bombing. I couldn't grasp it at first. I completely collapsed – he was my whole world. That day, I had felt something, even before I knew. I had been praying for my husband since the morning because a strange feeling made me sense his death. My heart was aching. I told them, I knew this in my heart, and then I didn't speak. He was very loved. My own mother used to say he was a son to her. She fell ill after his death. My husband was a civilian, he had nothing to do with politics. He was an exceptional man, loving and affectionate. I went home to say goodbye to him before they buried him. Did I say goodbye to him? Yes, I did. Then we buried him, under bombardment. Although the war was in its beginning, many people had no opportunity to bury their dead – the Israelis would bomb the mourners in the graveyard and then others would be killed, so people in Gaza would go to bury one person and end up burying more.

I went back to our house, despite the intense bombing. Our memories, mine and my husband's, were everywhere. I stayed until the afternoon. I could see him, he was right there in front of me, in every corner. I saw him clearly. I couldn't bear staying in the house without him, I saw his clothes and I couldn't bear it. Life is unendurable without him. So I went back to my family home and became displaced in their house. They were hard days, frightened for my children and not yet believing that my husband was dead. They tried to calm me but my heart would beat wildly and I was overwhelmed with terror. I would look at my children with fear. I would look at everything around me with fear.

We were gathered together in the family home. My older brother lived on the floor above us, and above him were my third and fourth brothers. My sister's husband had migrated to Iceland. She had a boy and girl, and had been staying with my family since her husband left, so her children also stayed with us. That night we had my

116

mother's eight grandchildren, we put them to bed all together.

The last thing I remember from that night was my mother shouting at us to stay in the room with her. My sister and I told her that we wanted to quiet the children, because they were being noisy and we didn't want to disturb her. Then suddenly I went flying through the air. That was 18 October. We were hugging our four youngest children in our laps and praying. Then I was flying right out of the house.

The smoke was black, the sky was red, burning red. I thought I was in a nightmare and would wake up, but that only lasted a second. I was holding my mobile phone, that's how I realized. Just one second. Then in the distance I saw a white ghost, a man. The world was night, and ghosts were white and red. They were relatives coming to save us, or trying to, but I couldn't understand anything. I was calling and shouting, screaming really, and I heard my own voice. A man I don't know came and asked me who I was, he had heard me as he was searching through the rubble, and he tried to pull me out. I was some distance from the site of the blast, the missile had sent me flying. That's how I survived, I wasn't buried completely under the rubble. They targeted us with two missiles, the first sent us flying, the second pulled the house down, it flattened the house. A vacuum bomb. The whole house fell down, every floor of it.

I couldn't feel anything. I couldn't feel or see very well, the dust was so thick, and all around me people were saving others. I could see them like ghosts, but they didn't see me, I was too far away. When I shouted they recognized me, and they saved me and took me to hospital. They performed surgery on me. The morning came and it was the next day. When I woke up and opened my eyes, I asked about my children and my family. They told me that my children were fine. I asked to see them, I didn't know anything, I was in so much pain, and instinct told me something had happened to them. My back was broken, my leg was wrapped up – I didn't yet know it had been cut off – my stomach was open, and my head was covered in stitches. Then my brother came to see me and told me my children had been martyred. I asked about my mother, he said she had died too. And his wife? He gave the same reply, she had died. My mother, my brother's wife, and our eight children.

Meanwhile, I went into surgery for an operation on my back; they found a fracture in my fifth vertebra. My injured brother, who had had both his legs amputated, had been poisoned by the toxic missiles. Those same missiles that cut off his legs didn't kill him straight away, but their poison killed him afterwards. He died right after his legs were amputated, following my mother, my children and my husband. That is how my family disappeared, as if they had never been. That is how they vanished from my side, and I didn't even have time to think. I was myself between life and death, I would wake up in agony only to pass out again.

Hana, my 27-year-old sister, mother to two children who died with my children – Hana raised her children alone. Because of economic reasons and unemployment, her husband had migrated abroad so he could work and make a decent life for them. She was next to me during the explosion and stayed with me in the hospital. She lost both her children. This is a photo of them, my sister's son was two and a half years old, he was called Nabil. His father was abroad when he was born, but he came to see Nabil when he was six months old. As for her daughter, Asil, she was born while he was away, and I think he never saw her at all. Overwhelming unemployment in Gaza forces men abroad to find work, so the rest of the family can live. Hana's husband didn't want to leave them, but he had no choice. He risked his life, he went through Turkey and Greece and across the sea like all refugees. We were frightened he would drown, but he survived and we were waiting for his affairs to be settled so my sister and her children could join him. But what happened while he was away happened, and his children died.

That ill-omened day never leaves me. 18 October, I will never forget it in all my life: the day the missile fell on us. I remember my sister and I praying the 'isha prayer, we were all in a state of fear and tension. We gathered together, all the siblings, the whole family. I remember we made dinner for our children. Yes, they ate. Alhamdulillah. They died with full stomachs, at least. The oldest was four years old, the others were two, a year and a half, and a few months old. The children would usually play, but that day they didn't, they didn't make a noise, they didn't make a sound. They went to sleep early, utterly exhausted from fear. We spent some time trying to entertain them and play with them, but the fear and anxiety were bigger than us, and bigger than them.

I remember remarking to my sister Hana that I had seen strange planes hovering overhead, a zannana of some kind, looping and turning around our house. I thought we were in danger and should get out of there. We were following the news, even though there was no internet – we charged our phones a bit whenever there was electricity, and the news brought more death, more loss of people we knew. Death was everywhere, everyone we knew was dying. I told myself we were going to die too. I could see death ahead of me, but no choices. Where would we go? I surrendered my life to God, and I said I am dying, my children and I, and I will stay with them and follow my husband. Then – yes! I remember the children were sleeping at that point, they were fast asleep. We went to check on them. There was another room which had a large window, I told my sister, let's go and get a bit of fresh air. That room had a balcony. My mother was lying down in the living room because we thought it was safer there. We were able to talk to each other. My older brother's wife, Hanin, and my brother Jihad, asked us to join them, they said – yes! I still remember! They said this phrase: 'Why is everyone sleeping in different places? Come here and join us, at least if we die, we die together.' Both of us, me and my sister, wanted to keep our children close, and so we decided to sleep and stay with the children in our arms to protect them, we enclosed them with our bodies. They were so soft and small. We put blankets over the whole floor so we could lie down, we actually fell asleep, and Hanin my brother's wife slept next to us. My mother was opposite us and she was calling out, 'Why are you going to sleep so early?' When my mother said that, I said, 'We'll put the children to sleep and come to you.' I am telling you about their deaths again. Yes, I want to tell it over and over.

During the first three days in hospital, my leg was wrapped in bandages and I didn't know what had happened to it. I didn't think it had been amputated, I thought that they were just changing the dressings and cleaning the wounds. I didn't feel much pain because my entire body was full of injuries and burns. I thought that my serious injury was my split head. Then I learned that my foot had been amputated from the heel down. They told me the wound was septic and had turned purple, and the poison would have spread through my body and killed me. Poisoning by missile was well-known, and in hospital, with a lack of medicine and basic medical equipment, the doctors were forced to keep patients alive by resorting to life-or-death choices – or put another way, the choice of cutting instead of dying. Bodies were being eaten away, people could see maggots swallowing their bodies. I saw maggots wriggling out of my wounds, I saw my body rotting while I was still alive. According to the doctors, the choice to amputate was my only chance of survival. Alhamdulillah, I lived.

The massacre of the al-Bakry family, that's what they call it. They were tiny children, little birds – they all died. I try to remember all of the dead. My husband's sister died as well. She was sheltering in Ma'an school, a school full of displaced people. She was killed there by a missile and her two sisters were with her as well, Rateel and Tarteel Abu al-Najaa. One was injured and the second died. By some miracle my other brother's pregnant wife was one of the survivors, her oldest son died and everyone thought she and her baby would die too. Although she had serious injuries – she had a broken neck and her spleen was removed – she survived and gave birth to a beautiful daughter, whom she named Intisar after my mother. It was a wonder we died and a wonder we lived. When my brother's wife woke up and saw her daughter next to her, she said, 'We will not be finished, we are going to live.'

I spent three months in the European Hospital, and my sister stayed with me. The bombing all around us was continuous. They had buried our children and our families. The hospital, like the other hospitals in the Gaza Strip, was full of displaced people alongside the injured, and the doctors and nurses. The bombing never stopped and wounded people continually arrived. Time was like pain, repeating itself the same way, incessantly. It wasn't clear to me, at first, that we were facing genocide. I thought it was a war that would pass like all the previous wars – some people would die and the rest would hold over until a future war, and calm would return. But after I saw the madness, the hospital becoming a horror site, the displaced people on top of each other, the bombing that never quietened, the moans of the injured repeating without pause... I used to tell myself that we would all die, they wouldn't leave a single one of us alive. The most hideous thing in the hospital was the lack of sedatives. Changing my dressings was torture, and all around us the displaced were hungry and sleeping in the corridors. The hospital was surrounded by Israeli tanks. And there was no water in the taps. Corpses would be brought in before our very eyes. An injured woman came, they said that all her family had been martyred, and she was placed in the room with us. Her back was completely open; I saw her insides. She stayed in the room like that for ten days, in front of us and in front of everyone, and then she died. I can't rid myself of the sight of her visible abdominal cavity. We saw terrible things, five cases entering together then leaving together, dead.

Under the barrage of bombs we would feel as though our heads were hovering in mid-air, incapable of describing the horrors we witnessed. Words seemed to fall short. Fear settled over us like a black shadow, and our family died, and those who were left were either injured or lost without trace. I would think of our children, those we hadn't seen, who were now under the soil. My head is still stuck in Gaza, as if the bombing is inside it right now, it never goes away. I always hear it and I experience it continually. My sister and I know no rest, we live as though we are under constant bombardment, our heads are filled with noise. I remember glass from the windows falling on top of us with every explosion, and how the ground would shake beneath us like a continual earthquake. Everything would shake and move around, the curtains were shredded, things overturned, as though the whole world was exploding all around us. We were surrounded by death and the bombing never stopped for a moment. We weren't even fortunate enough to have a chance to rest, we would stay awake, longing for sleep, even for a single hour. The bombs and missiles weren't the only problem; tanks lay siege to us, and zannanat filled the sky, and we were always waiting any moment for the bullet they might fire at us. We were swimming in bodies. Then they came and unleashed a fire belt around us in Khan Younis, in the European quarter, around the hospital, dozens of missiles all at once. Why did they bomb a hospital?

What was left of my family was displaced to Rafah. They lived in a tent, and my sister and I were in the hospital thinking about them and what was happening to them. After they bombed the hospital surroundings with a fire belt, we were frightened – there were tanks surrounding us, and we were hearing news of the other massacres in the Baptist, al-Shifa and Nasser [Hospitals]. Displaced people arrived and told us about mass graves. We knew their goal was the hospitals, and that we would end up in a mass grave too. The displaced people told us that some Israeli soldiers were entering the hospitals and stealing people's organs, even their skins; they said that this happened in Nasser. They were stories no rational mind could believe. They were killing indiscriminately, gathering up the sick and their carers and murdering them together. The displaced people told us all these awful things, and sometimes we saw them from the hospital windows. The Israeli soldiers were murdering individually, or rounding people up and killing them in one go. A woman said to an Israeli soldier, 'Stay away from me, I am pregnant,' and he beat her in her stomach with his rifle.

All this took place while my sister and I were in hospital, terrified, like all the rest of the people. I said to my sister, 'We have to get out.' Everything around us was destroyed, and the quadcopters were turning people all around into disfigured corpses, bodies left lying on the streets. No phrase can express the catastrophes we lived through, the terror that enveloped us like a thick black blanket.

Everything around us was collapsing. Through the windows, we could see scenes of death recurring like never-ending nightmares. They were murdering people in the most obscene ways, and horror pursued us at every instant. We were struck with profound dread. We couldn't stay in the hospital, so we decided to leave. Our only goal was to reach our family's tent in Rafah alive.

We arrived there, and my brother sent a car to pick us up, and we survived. But we had fled from one hell to another no less grim. We lived in a tent in the al-Mawasy area. There were no bathrooms, it was an area of tents with no hygiene facilities, the bathroom was shared by more than three hundred people, and our tent, which became a prison for us, was pitched on sand – it was impossible to move over it in a wheelchair. Yes, life in the camp was just as much of a nightmare. My wounds were inflamed, and my body suffered pain from cold at night and from sun during the day, without medicine, or a bed, or enough food.

We reached December. The camp was overflowing with thousands of people, there was no water, and prices were on fire. My two brothers would travel long distances to bring us water. And despite everything, we weren't safe even there – they were bombing Rafah as well. In the end, our family decided to leave the tent in Rafah and go back to our destroyed home, to pitch our tent on its rubble. The Israelis were everywhere, hunting us wherever we went, and the bombing never stopped.

Things haven't stopped, to the point that – I am frightened to say it – seeing dead bodies has become normal. Their worst atrocity was digging up the graves of the dead. People said that the Israeli soldiers were tearing up people's graves and taking out their bodies, and they dug up my children's graves and stole their bodies. Alhamdulillah, they left my husband's grave as it is, but they had no mercy on the graves of my children. They murdered them and wouldn't even leave them in peace even after their death. What do they want with the bodies of little children? What will they do with their bodies after killing them?

If I heard this story I wouldn't have believed it, but it happened to me. They stole my children's bodies. How can I sleep when my eyes are full of questions: Where are my children's remains? Why did they steal their bodies after killing them? How will my mind ever be quiet when I don't know where they are? I spend hours every night wondering about their fate, and this question tears me apart from inside: Where are my children? Where are their remains now?

MUHAMMAD ALAA ABDELAAL QARMOUT
16 years old
Jabalia Camp

I was at home on 5 November with my large family: my brothers and sisters, my mother and father, my father's sister, and her children. That day, they bombed our house. They had already bombed close by, but we didn't leave. We stayed till that day, when they bombed us and all my family died. All of them died. Only I survived. We were asleep, it was around midnight when the bombing began.

I woke up two days later.

I found myself in the Indonesian Hospital.

My mother's name was Tahrir Eisa Abd al-Razzaq al-Kurdi – my mother died. And my siblings, Basma, Munira, Mahyideen, Ezzeddine, Maryam – they all died. My aunt and her children died as well. My grandmother and grandfather. That missile killed fifteen members of my family.

I can't tell you about anything straight after the bombing, because I wasn't conscious. I can't remember. I woke up in the hospital with burns, part of my spleen removed, and I couldn't move my feet.

When I woke up in the Indonesian Hospital, it was under siege from the Israelis. I stayed there until the end of the siege, and I was the last one to leave the hospital. I didn't know, then, the extent of the massacre around me. No one told me my family had died. I was in a desperate condition, and my aunts and uncles on both sides would say to me that my family were injured and would come soon. I didn't get it! I couldn't understand what had happened. I was insisting on seeing them, so they told me that my family was displaced to Fallujah. I asked and asked, and they said they were in al-Shifa Hospital. Every morning I asked about them, and I would ask again in the afternoon, and all through the night, but there was no reply. Sometimes I was silent for days, then I would ask again. I constantly insisted on seeing them. I would demand the doctor answer me. Later, I learned that they had forbidden anyone to tell me what had happened. Everyone knew my family had died, apart from me. Every day I woke up and asked, I never lost hope.

In the hospital, they categorized my case as critical and severe. My whole body was burned, even my face. My face was burned and I had no features left. They thought I would die. My eyes were closed; I couldn't see clearly out of my right and I couldn't see from my left eye at all. Even now, I am still having operations to restore my features. I remember they used to give me just a drop of water. I could hear them saying that I would die soon, I wasn't unconscious as they thought. I heard lots of things, and every time one of them came to take a look at me, I was scared they would take me to the morgue. I lived through the siege, but I don't actually remember much of it, my brain was confused.

I remember some details. I remember them saying that the bombing would stop and there was a ceasefire on the way. I had known that we were under siege, hemmed in by tanks and constant bombing. I wasn't saying anything, but I relaxed a little when I heard there was a ceasefire. But what happened was the opposite. The bombing started up again. I felt bullets hit the wall behind me. We were learning that we couldn't move. And I couldn't do a thing, even seeing was a struggle. They besieged us, then they entered.

True, I couldn't see, but I heard everything clearly, noises coming from a shadowy world. My eyes were closed, but I heard bullets thudding and bombs exploding and screams of pain and moaning. I heard people moving around me, because hearing continued to be the only means I had of connecting with the outside world. When they brought me out of the hospital, they put me on the steps of the bus. The ambulances and buses were crammed full, so I was told, and so I could feel. I could smell wounds and people, and I could feel bodies bumping into each other. At last we set off, then we arrived at Netzarim checkpoint, and they stopped the buses and searched us. Then they took me and some others off the bus, and they put me on the ground. I stayed lying down, while the others left and headed towards the checkpoint. As I've told you, I couldn't see, I couldn't walk and I couldn't speak. I could only lie prone on the ground. I felt the soldiers walking around us, and I could hear their boots clearly. I heard gunshots, and I heard they killed some people and arrested others. We stayed like that for hours, then they took us to Nasser Hospital.

I stayed in Nasser Hospital. The bombing carried on all the time, and the siege there was just like the siege at the Indonesian Hospital. We had to leave because the Israelis were on the brink of storming this hospital as well. There was a huge number of patients. I had operation after operation; I can't remember any more why I was always in surgery. When the Israeli army entered Khan Younis, some of the doctors and people fled, then the Israelis bombed the hospital. A few of the doctors and patients stayed behind under bombardment that never stopped, I heard them saying it was vital that I have continuous operations otherwise I would die from gangrene in my feet. My eyes also needed operations, and so did my burned hands.

My uncle discharged me from hospital, he said they would destroy the building, and actually they bombed it as soon as I left. My uncle told me that the missile landed in the room where I had been sleeping, and all the patients there died.

My father was a physics teacher, and we were happy. I remember being asleep when the bombing happened. I used to think, without knowing why, that even though people were dying, and despite the bombing all around, we would be all right. I don't know why we weren't afraid. I don't know why we stayed.

I went to sleep, and I woke up to find my life had turned upside down. My whole life vanished, and I couldn't understand it. They lied to me at first and didn't tell me the truth. They waited for two months, because they were afraid for me, then they told me. I remember my uncle asking me, 'Who has not spoken to you or checked on you?' I said, 'Ummi.' And he said, 'Your mother was martyred.' Then he asked again, 'Who else?' I said, 'Abi.' And he said, 'Your father was martyred.' Then he asked again, 'Who else?' So I asked after my aunt, and he replied, 'She was martyred.' That was how I learned of their deaths, one after another. I asked about my grandfather, and he said, 'Your grandfather had a heart attack and died, too. They were defeated.'

I forgot everyone around me. I forgot my friends. I've forgotten so much. I've only just started to remember a little. I can't remember my family's faces. When I saw photos of them I remembered some of their features, but not very clearly. I try to remember, but my memory is weak.

I want to go back to Gaza. I am the only one left of my family and my uncle is there, there's no doubt in my mind that I'll return. Part of my spleen was removed and I survived, even though they thought I wouldn't, or that I would ever see again.

I remember that I've had many operations on my eyes and on parts of my burned body. I also remember those torn bodies, the martyrs around me – that sight was the hardest to absorb. It feels as though what happened wasn't real, as though I myself am not real, and I say Alhamdulillah, but how is it everyone has died?

We used to live a normal life, we were young. My older brother was studying electrical engineering, and as for me, I dreamed of becoming a vet. My little sister Maryam, she was 4 years old. I loved her so much. Everyone died. My aunt's daughters – Rahaf, Sara and Dima – they all died as well.

I am trying to remember, but I don't remember very well.

Yes, I remember that we didn't want to leave our house, because all of Gaza was being bombed and there was no safe place. I remember that I have forgotten a lot of my life from before the injury. As for what I remember about life after the injury, it's from what people have told me. I remember a little of our life as a family. Some pictures come to my mind, but I don't really understand what the words mean. I only remember that I used to want to study veterinary medicine, and that I used to love animals, perhaps.

SAJA YASIR SALIH
23 years old
Deir al-Balah

I was the happiest woman in the world, that is truly what I used to feel. My husband, Yaaqoub al-Arqan, was the kindest person anyone could possibly meet. He was young, 29 years old, extraordinarily handsome, kind beyond description. He worked as a mandi chef. Yes! Mandi, the famous Yemeni dish. I married him three years ago, I loved him more than any other being, I loved him more than I ever loved anyone. Affectionate, generous, honourable, with an innate talent for making the house overflow with love and understanding and contentment, so perfect you felt he was an alien, that he wasn't of this earth. He filled my life, and I was prepared to give him my entire life without a shred of hesitation. My life with him was bliss. I lived with him in a building where the apartments were distributed among his family: his parents, his uncles, his brothers and their wives and children, and us. Ten families lived in the same building. God blessed me with a daughter we named Mira. Her life stopped at the age of a year and seven months. When the war began, I was pregnant with Sham and I was intending to teach after giving birth, as I had studied English Language at university and I loved assisting my husband in our daily lives. It wasn't easy to find work, as openings were few. I knew someone who had graduated before me and hadn't found a professional opportunity yet, so I was thinking of opening a private language institute, and until that time I would often help my husband in the kitchen.

I gave birth to my daughter Sham in my family home in Nuseirat Camp. That was at the end of November, there was bombing everywhere in the camp. I couldn't stay away from my husband so I decided to go home at once, despite the danger. Sham and I miraculously escaped death, and when she was two weeks old, and I was still postpartum, I took her to the clinic for a tuberculosis vaccination. On our way home, the bombing reached our neighbourhood, al-Borouk, in Deir al-Balah. I saw it! At first, I thought the missiles had fallen on our house. I ran towards it like a madwoman, and I hugged my daughter Mira, thanking God she was all right. The glass in the house was shattered, its doors and windows were blown off, and it was filled with black smoke that had a strange, horrible smell. Everyone said these missiles were equipped with poison. I couldn't rule this out – the smoke made breathing difficult and painful, you felt it slicing your insides with every breath, it gave you a terrible cough and headache. But the missile didn't hit our building directly, it fell on our neighbour's house, our neighbour from the Matar family. I remember eight of them were killed straight away, the moment the bomb hit. Our house was in a terrible state, but having decided to stay no matter what, my husband and I began to clean it up, side by side. It took us the entire day, from morning till evening. We removed shrapnel and dust and filth, while our neighbours brought out their dead.

I don't deny that those days after 7 October were extremely challenging, but with my husband and my two daughters beside me, my hardships were eased. It was enough that we were all right and together – then I could overcome every horror. That evening, after the bombing, our bodies were wracked with exhaustion but the house was once again clean, tidy and habitable. We decided to stay put no matter what, we had lived in it and we would die in it. And anyway, where would we go? I was still postpartum, Sham was barely two weeks old, it was winter and the weather was cold. We were going to stay. At the end of that exhausting day, my husband said, 'I'm hungry, make us some dinner.' I was in the kitchen preparing food, Mira was with her grandmother who lived in the same building, and my husband was lying down, waiting for the food, when they hit us with two missiles. It was night-time and the internet was cut off – we had gotten used to them doing this whenever they wanted to bomb a certain area. They wanted to kill us away from the eyes of the world. They hit us with two missiles, one at the top of the building and one at its base, as if they wanted to ensure that no one stood a chance of survival. The kitchen was located in a side corner, slightly raised from the principal building, and when I was inside I saw the flash of a missile and heard its whine. In a split second, I saw a quick flash and heard a piercing sound and said, 'Ash-hada an la ilaha illa Allah'* and the explosion rang out. Everything happened in the blink of an eye. The blast sent me flying some distance, and both missiles destroyed the entire building. The whole building collapsed to the ground. In that strike, twenty people were killed at once, including my husband and my two daughters, and seven others were severely injured. My husband died hungry. Whenever I think of that, I can feel my heart shattering. And I was underneath the rubble, far away from the bombsite. I thought I was about to die of suffocation. Above me was wreckage, there was smoke in my chest, and from below came the screams of women and children who were buried further down. I couldn't shout, or breathe, then all at once I felt a gush of air enter my lungs. I kept thinking of my husband and daughters,

* The first part of the shahada, the Muslim declaration of faith, 'I bear witness that there is no god but God.'
  It is considered a virtuous act to say the shahada as your last words.

and I hoped, with all faith and certainty, that God would kill me and take me with them if they had been martyred. With that, I closed my eyes, certain that I would never open them again. I was in darkness beneath the debris, thinking of my family, and I could hear screaming and groaning when the air entered my lungs and I breathed. I found myself completely buried, but I saw a very small gap I could pass my fingers through. I couldn't believe I was still alive, I couldn't believe I hadn't died. I pushed my fingers out of the hole and began fluttering them, hard at first, then feebly, as once again I realized what a struggle it was to breathe, how near death I was. They must have seen my fingers because they began digging to pull me out, four young men digging with their bare hands. They had no tools or machinery to dig, and no electricity or power to operate them if they had, but they dug until they got me out. I am sure they were horrified at first, when they saw my leg lying on my stomach. One of them took out my leg first, it swung in his hand like a rag, then they pulled the rest of me out. After that they put me on a bed-spread, a bit like a primitive stretcher, and walking first among the piles of rubble, then running.

I am aware of everything that happened throughout that time. I couldn't speak, I had to make do with pointing them to where my husband and daughters were, so they would go to them and help them. The four young men took me to the street, where they put me on a mattress on the ground. I wasn't alone, there were dozens of bodies surrounding me, to right and left and in every direction, bodies of the injured and bodies of the killed, corpses. I couldn't feel any pain yet, actually I didn't feel anything, no fear and nothing else either. I was only thinking of my husband and daughters, I wanted to be reassured about them. In the street – while I was among the bodies lined up next to each other – they wrapped my leg in a bandage then took me to al-Aqsa Hospital. 11 December, how can I forget the day they bombed us? The hospital was in a catastrophic state, with injured people everywhere, and the Reception Department filled with yet more. Once again they put me on the ground, in between dozens of bodies left lying there, and underneath dozens of bodies that walked or were passed over us. I saw people who had lost their limbs, others whose bodies were torn to pieces, others whose stomachs and heads were open. An intense crush of people, chaos, screaming and agony everywhere, the medical staff unable to accommodate the number of casualties. They said my injury was trivial. Yeah, I swear to God! My leg was severed and my bare bone was sticking out into the air and my injury was considered one of the minor ones. They were right – my injury wasn't among the most dangerous that demanded urgent intervention. So in the moment, they made do with putting some antiseptic on my leg and went off to care for the rest of the injured. Then I heard them mention some names. They mentioned the name of my husband's father, Abu Ibrahim Yaaqoub al-Arqan, and his wife Faiza, in a list of the martyrs. Then I remembered that my daughter Mira was with her grandmother when the bomb hit, while I was preparing dinner in the kitchen. In that instant, I was able to speak. I screamed with all the power I had, 'Was my daughter with them?' No one replied. I said to myself, 'If her grandmother died, then surely Mira died alongside her.' Then our neighbour walked in between the bodies, he was a friend of my husband, I said to him, 'Go to my husband and daughters and check on them.' But I didn't hear any news from him. It emerged later that because of the intensity of the bombardment and the difficulties in the recovery operations, they were only able to finish bringing the bodies out in the morning.

My father told me that my husband and daughters were fine, and I would see them after I recovered, but what was important now was that I have an operation. They amputated my leg and stitched up half the wounds in my weakened body, leaving the other half open, and I began my journey of pain and sedatives. The agony was horrific; it had me screaming and crying. My breasts turned to stone, my chest was full of milk for Sham. Pain upon pain accumulated; the pain of my amputation, the pain of the wounds, the pain in my chest hard as stone, the pain of missing my husband and daughters. Why didn't they come to me? Why couldn't I see them? Why couldn't I put Sham on my breast and feed her? I kept screaming and blacking out then waking up, asking about my husband. 'Your husband is in intensive care and in critical condition,' said my father. 'Be a little patient and the hardness in your chest will gradually get better,' said my mother. I didn't believe it, I wasn't convinced, my heart wasn't reassured – at least give me Sham so she can nurse! My mother said my daughter was fine, but it wasn't safe to bring a two-week-old infant to a hospital brimming with germs, she might catch a serious infection. A week passed, my father saw that I was recovering a little, and he began to be able to say to me bluntly, in a few words, 'Your husband and daughters were martyred, Alhamdulillah.' I repeated after him, 'Alhamdulillah.' My beloved husband Yaaqoub, loved by all who knew and met him, the kindest man in the world, was dead. Mira, the little soul who was playing happily in her grandmother's lap, was dead. Sham, whose presence the world couldn't bear for more than a fortnight, and for whom my chest was full of milk, waiting for her, was dead. Alhamdulillah.

Since I learned of their deaths, I have not stopped

thinking of them for one moment. I haven't stopped, not for a single moment, going over and over the possibility they could have survived. The Israelis bomb the bulldozers taking part in the digging and rescue operations. They bomb the ambulances trying to save the wounded. They bomb roads and clinics and hospitals. They keep doing this, continuously. It if weren't for that, wouldn't there have been a chance of saving more souls? Wouldn't it have been possible that my husband and daughters could have survived? Isn't it conceivable that there was a spark of life left in them while they were beneath the rubble, and they could have been saved if there had been digging equipment available? They were my entire life. I kept thinking of them when I was lying on my hospital bed, remembering every moment we lived together, and I felt my soul tearing itself from my body. I couldn't stop crying, sedatives would calm my pain a little so I would fall asleep, only to wake in horror at the fact my family had disappeared. All the people who died in that bombing, they are buried in a single pit, a mass grave. They weren't even able to bring out all the bodies, some martyrs from the family remained in the wreckage. And not all the retrieved corpses were whole – some had limbs severed, they were just pieces of flesh in various sizes. I thank God fervently that the bodies of my husband and daughters were intact. I console myself that they weren't left under the rubble, they didn't turn to dust, they weren't brought out in shreds. They were brought out whole, and buried in the same shape that God created them in, in the best of forms.*

While I was in hospital, we were still threatened with bombs and quadcopters. These last were helicopter-drones, small-sized, known as flying killers. It felt like

* Qur'an 95:4.

they were living among us. It's not true they were only for photography and surveillance, they used them to kill us too. It was quadcopters that killed two of my husband's aunts and some of our friends. Horrifying creatures, mechanical murderers, beasts designed to kill – quite simply, they used these drones to hunt us. What do they want? I know what I don't want: I don't want to be homeless, I don't want to live in a tent, so we stayed. If we had left, would it even have been possible to come back? We know families who left decades ago, after the Israelis drove them out, and they still haven't returned. And because we were attached to our land, they decided to kill us. They have bombed everything: homes, schools, hospitals, water and fuel reservoirs – everything. They have killed many people, mostly women and children. I don't believe the official numbers, the real numbers will be revealed in the coming days and they will be much greater. Everything I am saying, no one has told to me, I didn't hear it on the news. I saw it and lived it all myself. They say they want to get rid of Hamas, then you see them bombing ambulances and tents, refuge centres for the displaced, schools and hospitals. And to do that, they use every weapon available to them. Planes drop loads that wipe out entire residential buildings in seconds, tanks bomb at random, they use phosphorus gas, and missiles equipped with poisons that we're not familiar with, but we suffer from their effects and their symptoms.

I want the whole world to know. My daughters, Mira al-Arqan, one year and seven months old. Sham al-Arqan, two weeks old. Now, they are birds in heaven. My husband's name: Yaaqoub al-Arqan. The Israelis murdered Yaaqoub and his two daughters. The Israelis murdered the kindest man in the world, the best husband on the face of the earth.

ABDULLAH YOUSEF AAKILA
13 years old
Al-Shati Camp

My father is a restaurant manager alongside his work as
a photojournalist. As for my mother, she completed a
degree in Arabic. I have a little brother who is 6 years old,
my older brother is 22 and my sister is 19. We used to live
together as a family, happily and honourably. At dawn on
7 October, I heard rockets being fired from Gaza. People
thought that Palestine was going to be liberated, I listened
to their conversations even though I didn't fully understand. Then war broke out, the Israelis began killing us
and displacing us. My family stayed in our house, we
didn't leave despite the non-stop bombing. The Israelis
arrived at a street close to us, they were bombing houses
without stopping and dropping leaflets demanding that
we leave the north and head to the south. In the end, we
decided to go to my uncle's house in the al-Sahaba district, in eastern Gaza. We went there, but the bombing
didn't stop, and the situation wasn't really any different.
But because our house was close to the border with the
Israelis, my family preferred to move to my uncle's house.
Life there was very hard. I used to walk a long way to get
drinking water, I collected water for my family every day.
At my uncle's, there were more than forty-five people
in one building with a shortage of food and water, and
the electricity was cut off. We just about managed to get
through the days, until they announced a ceasefire, of
– seven days? Did it last longer than that? I don't fully
remember the details of that time.

My mind is muddled. What I do remember, clearly,
is that the bombing never stopped. I saw buildings collapsing all around. We lived under this constant fear.

The bombing wasn't normal, they used fire belts, the destruction was horrendous. I was frightened but I didn't say so in front of my family, to help them keep calm. At the beginning of the ceasefire, my father decided that we wouldn't leave the house, no matter what, even if the Israeli army made a ground invasion of the area. My sister was afraid, she was crying and wanted to leave, and in the end my father agreed because the news confirmed that the ground invasion was coming, and the Israelis were killing everyone they came across. We decided to leave on the last day of the ceasefire. At seven in the morning, the bombing started and we left the house.

My older brother stayed behind with my uncle in al-Shati Camp, as my uncle insisted on staying in his house until he died and my brother refused to leave him. My mother was determined to leave, but at the same time she was very scared. I wanted to stay with my brother, but I didn't say anything. I'm the younger son, one look from my mother would have been all it took to make me keep quiet and go with them. We would have left in any case because the Israelis issued clear directives that whoever stayed would be killed. We packed our things, me and my uncles and aunts, and we got on a bus belonging to UNRWA. There were sixteen of us on a bus with a United Nations logo and flag on it. My father opted to stay with my disabled grandmother and said he would follow us in the second group. That's how we left my father and went on alone.

We got on the bus and set off. The bombing never stopped. They told us that UNRWA buses wouldn't be bombed, but I could see and hear bombs all around. I remember shaking with fear, the war was besieging us from every side. When we reached Palestine Stadium, we were bombed. Children and women were inside the bus. The driver was an UNRWA employee. It wasn't just one bomb that landed on us, but several. Everyone burned, my uncles, my mother, my whole family. I was in the middle of the bus where the missile fell, I saw red flooding everything. I remember I began to smack my body, I didn't pass out, I starting slapping my burned face. I thought it was a nightmare and I wanted to wake up, but it wasn't. Everything happened in the blink of an eye. The fire was huge and the explosion enormous.

We had brought some of our furniture with us, as well as a gas canister and a can of petrol. When they bombed us, the whole bus exploded. I saw my mother on fire right in front of me. I heard her say the shahada, and my sister died the same way, right there. I saw her burning. My uncle's wife and daughter were burned up too, there was a solid wall of fire inside the bus. There was a sniper behind us, and a quadcopter above us – the sniper shot at the burning bus and the drone bombed us. There were sixteen people in the bus. Four died, and the remaining twelve of us were alive, but badly burned.

I remember we walked, suffering from extreme burns, until we came to an ambulance. The strike was so intense I hadn't felt any pain at first, but the pain began when we got into the ambulance. That was 4 December. I tried to comfort my little brother who was 6 years old, telling him, 'It's a game,' trying to cheer him up. They took us to the Baptist Hospital, but there wasn't any medicine or anything that could help us. My face was burned and swollen and had turned black, my brother was unconscious. The hospital didn't seem like a hospital at all. My face was agony, and when I saw myself I was horrified. My little brother Jad was even worse off, his leg was broken in three places and he was badly burned. When my father arrived at the hospital, he didn't recognize me at first. They told him, 'This is your son!' He looked at me, completely stunned. Then he went to see my brother and came back in tears. He told me that later on. I struggled to hear what was going on, and the pain was tearing me apart. My little brother was constantly asking for water, and my father would just look at him, eyes full of anguish. I could only see from the corner of my eye. My brother Jad was a burned-up fleshy lump. I heard him asking for his mother. I couldn't really understand what was happening. The next day, when my father took Jad's hands, they were cold. The doctor said my brother had died. I could hardly hear what was happening, the pain was killing me, the burns on my face and body and the painful shrapnel stopped me from thinking at all. I couldn't say goodbye to my brother like I wanted to. After my brother's death and burial, my father went back to the site of the burned-out bus. My mother, my sister, my uncle's wife and her daughter had remained there, burning all night. No one had been able to get close to the bus because of the non-stop bombing and the snipers. Even so, when Jad died and they buried him, my father decided – he told me later – to go back there despite the danger, to take the corpses of my mother, sister and family out of the bus. When he found them, they had completely turned to coal. They buried my mother, my sister, my uncle's wife and her daughter in a single shroud. My father told me there wasn't enough left of them to fill even that, just some small, charred lumps. So they buried them like that, together, body parts charred by fire and destruction.

After burying them, my father came back to me. The pain was getting worse and worse, and there were no painkillers, and I hadn't seen my face yet. It was later on that I discovered I was this deformed. The burns were intense, the pain was unbearable. The worst thing in life

142

is burns. I had third- and fourth-degree burns. My father spent days looking for burns medication. There were nine of us suffering from severe burns, but we were discharged from the hospital because it was no use us staying there. There was no medication, no painkillers, not even any beds for us and nowhere we could stay.

My father kept searching until finally he managed to track down gauze and some medical solutions. We began to smell our bodies decomposing, that was unbearable torture. We went back to al-Shati Camp, to our house. We didn't have anywhere else to go, so we went back to the place we had fled from. My father tried to treat our wounds, but what with the continual bombing, and the lack of medicine and food and drink, we all felt we were going to die. But the biggest fear was rot, that our bodies were rotting. I wished I would die then and there; I began praying for it.

I thought the bombing would kill us, I expected death, but it didn't come. In the end, my father decided that we would go to the Rafah crossing, to try and save me. He said we had to walk there, he had a journalist friend who wanted to help me get treated. This friend told us to leave between nine in the morning and two in the afternoon, but people warned us off, saying we'd be killed by bombs or snipers. Even so, my father was determined. We set off walking. Someone took us south, to the mosque in Sheikh Ijlin, then my father and I went on foot, carrying a white flag. I was covered all over in burns and I couldn't understand how I was even able to walk. I was afraid of the sun, but the sky was cloudy, so we kept going. We passed an Israeli checkpoint. We walked for hours, the bombing carried on all around us – we saw terrible things. My father was carrying four bags and a white flag. We arrived at last after crossing Wadi Gaza and my aunt's son came to take us to the border crossing.

I still don't understand what happened to us. The flag on the bus was blue, the UNRWA flag. I thought they wouldn't bomb a bus that belonged to the United Nations. But I was wrong. Why did the sniper shoot at burned corpses? Why did the zannanat bomb the bus again? I'm still young, so they say, I'm 13 and a half now, but I understand a lot. I saw the dead and wounded, the hardest part was seeing people who had lost limbs. I can't describe the pain I felt. I'm not a kid any more. What does it mean, that I've lost my family? What does it mean, that my brother Jad died from burns that way? I saw my mother on fire with my own eyes. I tried to save her, but the electric door wouldn't open. The driver escaped and I wasn't able to open the door. My uncle threw his son out of the window, and I survived because my uncle eventually managed to get the door open, but the missile had fallen right on my mother and my sister and they burned, they were in the part where the missile landed.

I was born in war, and the bombing we experienced seemed 'normal' to me. It never occurred to me that they would burn us up like that. I've seen war before, I thought I was used to bombs. There aren't any children in Gaza, we grow old before our time. My face is burned, my entire body is full of shrapnel. I can't speak about the pain. It's indescribable. There was no sedation, I lived through every bit of agony, and now I know exactly what hell is. I hoped I would die, but I didn't. They say I'm a kid! I don't understand what that means. Now I think of my brother who is still in Gaza. I know my burned face will never go back to normal. I used to be so happy and good-looking.

HUDA SUFYAN SAEED AL-BAGHDADY
33 years old
Gaza City

On Friday 6 October, we were at home in our neighbourhood of Tel al-Hawa, having a party for my brother's
graduation. After that, the family went to sleep, but I
had to go back to work on a university project. Though
I already have a certificate in classroom teaching, I'm
also studying architectural engineering. At half past six
in the morning, everyone was woken by the rockets that
Hamas fired, and all we could do was wait for the Israeli
response. We reckoned there would be bombing that
wouldn't last more than a few days, we never imagined
what would engulf us, so we decided to stay. And anyway,
where would we go? How could we leave our homes?
Who would look after them? The bombing intensified,
we were surrounded by fire belts that made the house
tremble, and we trembled too. My sister was displaced
from Abraj al-Mukhabarat with her husband and four
children and they came to stay with us. We wouldn't have
left had we not got a call from my brother. He was living
in Turkey, he called us and insisted that we get out. He
said that things would not stop at bombing, there was
going to be a ground invasion, they would attack, so we
absolutely had to leave. We no longer had a choice. We
left the house in ten minutes, we packed a small suitcase
for everyone, each of us put in two pieces of underwear,
and we left. We weren't alone, people filled the streets and
the bombing was constant. Four vehicles belonging to the
Red Cross had turned up. We discovered they wanted
us to leave for the south in convoys, in accordance with
Israeli directives. People didn't want to do that, but what
else could we do when the bombing never stopped and

our houses were crumbling before our eyes and massacres were everywhere? Death fell on us from the sky, and soon it would reach us over land with the start of the ground invasion. What about the children? The Israelis forced us out. I have a sister living in Khan Younis and a grandmother in Rafah. I have six brothers and four sisters, some are married with families, some are abroad. We went to my grandmother's house in Rafah. There, we found ourselves in the same danger. We stayed in Rafah, going to sleep and waking up to the sound of bombing and the names of massacres and the numbers of martyrs. Where could we escape to? Should we throw ourselves into the sea?

In my grandmother's house, we stayed on the ground floor of a six-storey building. The situation in Rafah wasn't easy, there was no water, no electricity and prices were high, but we managed, Alhamdulillah. I still remember how we were the night the building was bombed, on 21 October. At first, I laid out blankets for me and my four-year-old son in the living room, trying to sleep. Then my sister and her children came to join us. After that, I picked up my son and went to my grandmother's room. Each of us would sleep a little in one room before moving to another, as if we were fleeing death. In my grandmother's room, I recited the prayer of Younis (peace be upon him) when he was in the belly of the whale, and I repeated the prayer until it got to three o'clock in the morning and I hadn't slept. I went to check on my brothers in their room, and I found them asleep. I sat on a chair, I said, I will stay like this and recite the Qur'an. I thought I was protecting them with my prayers and my recitation. I must have dozed off without realizing, because when I woke up I found myself in the middle of wreckage. I didn't feel anything and I didn't hear the explosion. I woke up and found myself in debris, in the dark, I could hear my brothers shouting and there was a choking smell of gunpowder. Perhaps it was four o'clock. They always bomb when people are asleep. The ceiling fell on my brother's three children and killed them at once.

I caught a glimpse of my brothers on the sofa and I began looking for my son. A man came to rescue me, there was shrapnel in every part of my body. I yelled, 'Don't rescue me! Rescue my family!' In the street, I could only see people's corpses, flung all over the place. They took limbs and torn up bodies out of the building, I saw them bringing out my uncle who had been martyred. I saw my sister's daughter and my uncle's daughter both alive. My mind was absorbed in counting the losses. There were twenty-four of us. I kept turning round and round, searching for survivors. When I saw my son, I hugged him and they took us to Abu Yousef Najjar Hospital. We call it a hospital, but really it's more of a clinic. They looked at my wounds and it was clear they weren't dangerous. Feeling thirsty, I drank water as though I hadn't drunk for years. I saw my mother. She seemed utterly traumatized. She was like a stone statue with glazed eyes. I saw my sister, her head was injured and bleeding and she kept asking about her children. Her husband, Muhammad al-Areer, whispered to me, 'The children are dead.' He said that and went silent. Lana, 12 years old; Muhammad, 10 years old; Zayd, 6 years old – the children of Muhammad al-Areer and Hala al-Baghdady were all killed in the bombing. I lied to my sister Hala and said to her, 'They're fine.' 'Where are they?' A nurse saved me from the dilemma of replying, she came to tell me that my two brothers were in a challenging state and were being moved to the European Hospital. I said, 'I'm going with them.' We left in three ambulances – along with both my brothers, they were taking my uncle, my uncle's son and my sister. My uncle's wife had lost her mind: she kept saying she was scraping off the meat, removing it from the stone, she was gathering up body parts and flesh and congealed blood from among the rubble and she didn't know who any of it belonged to or who each part should be returned to. She screamed, 'Impossible! Impossible they've become body parts! Impossible we are dying like this!'

As soon as we arrived at the European Hospital they took my uncle and my brother Abdullah to surgery, and the rest stayed in the Reception Department. The hospital was suffering from a lack of doctors, equipment and medicine. My other brother Bara was in a terrible state – the right-hand side of his face had disappeared, his fingers had gone flying, he had shrapnel embedded all over his body, his bones were sticking out, his hands were crushed, he had been torn to pieces while still alive. When I saw him, he just said calmly, 'My hands hurt.' Those words proved to me he was alive. He would stay like that for three days, his case was challenging, but he was better off – so the doctors asserted – than other injured people, and so he could wait. In the face of dwindling human and medical resources, the doctors were forced to triage and prioritize, to choose cases that were most critical and in need of immediate intervention. A difficult thing. As for Ibrahim, my other uncle's 12-year-old son, he was now on his own – his whole family was dead. That made nine martyrs.

They brought my brother Abdullah out of the operating room and rushed him to intensive care. I saw them running with him, his tongue dangling from his mouth, his dressings leaking blood and falling on the ground.

I stayed with my brother Bara. His temperature went up to the forties and stayed like that for a month. His body was torn to shreds, as I told you, and his many wounds became infected, and he lost a lot of blood. With the lack of medicine, naturally his temperature remained high. I would look at him, absolutely incredulous at what my eyes were seeing, I could hardly make out the brother I knew. Apparently, the missile fell close to him, so it mutilated him but didn't kill him. I went to Dr Saad al-Salwat, I told him that that my brother was slipping away from us, his temperature was high and he was turning blue. They gave him four units of blood and a shot of paracetamol in his vein to lower his temperature. Transferring a single unit of blood to him took two hours, and I spent those hours at his side, putting compresses on him. At one point, I was wracked with exhaustion while sitting with him and I dozed off briefly, only to wake up from a terrifying nightmare that made me rush to the care ward to examine my brother Abdullah. That's how I was in the hospital, moving back and forth between my brothers. I had become nurse to both, because of the lack of nursing staff. All the while, I was in a state of constant anxiety about my children, the oldest was 13. They stayed in al-Mawasy Camp in Rafah with their father. They were fine, I told myself, they will be fine, and I cannot leave the hospital. My mother still had her stone look, I hadn't told her about the deaths of my uncle and his wife but she realized it by herself. I knew when I saw her leaving the hospital when they were burying the family's martyrs. She prayed over them and said goodbye to her brother in silence.

Finally, after a long wait, Bara went into surgery. They cleaned his wounds, extracted shrapnel from his body and amputated his fingers. At first, I was delighted, because he hadn't lost a whole limb and it was only a matter of fingers, but afterwards he had successive surgeries, a new operation every day. Meanwhile the bombing continued, and the throngs of new wounded arrivals to the hospital never stopped, forcing us to wait for his turn every time. The hospital filled up with corpses, with displaced people, with the injured and their carers. We were piled up on top of each other, there were even days when my mother and I would sleep on Bara's bed.

All of a sudden, Bara's health deteriorated. His wounds rotted, his dressings turned black and every day when I changed his sheets they would be drenched with blood. Once, I even woke up to the sound of blood dripping from his bed onto the floor. Bara was bleeding heavily, swimming in blood. There were no more units of blood available, so I had to search for donors, while my mother remained a statue with glazed eyes. Equally, I wasn't content to care for my brother and just ignore the other patients. How could I stand there and cross my arms when I saw injured people with no one to care for them? I found myself moving from this one to that. I became a nurse for everyone, and this work, combined with anxiety and little sleep, put me in a state of permanent exhaustion.

On 29 October, I went to the care ward to check on Abdullah, and I was in very low spirits. Perhaps my constant preoccupation with Bara, with securing the units of blood he needed, had distracted me from Abdullah. I greeted him and spoke to him, and then the doctor asked me to leave. I refused, I was determined to stay with him. I kept reciting the Qur'an next to him, asking God to be merciful and grant him death. Imagine it! Wallahi, I love him so much, but I hoped he would die. He had been placed on artificial breathing apparatus, his blood pressure was dropping, he was gradually turning blue. He was no longer my handsome brother in the flower of youth. Again, the doctor insisted that I leave. From her insistence, I understood that Abdullah was passing, but I absolutely refused. I stayed by his side, watching the monitor screen until the equipment let out his last sigh. When another doctor came to cover his face, I yelled at him, 'Don't suffocate my brother!' He was dead and all I could think of was that he would suffocate. I was losing my mind. I kept standing there, stroking his body, repeating, Alhamdulillah, Alhamdulillah.

The hospital wasn't a safe place, neither was the school. I left once to buy coffee beans – a single spoonful was ten shekels – and I saw them bringing in the victims of a bombing on a school that was sheltering displaced people. I stood at the entrance to the emergency ward, watching them bringing in the wounded, the dead, the human body parts in paper bags. It was appalling to see. Fifteen people were killed in that bombing, dozens wounded. Unfortunately, the hospital was so full the doctors had to put my brother Bara in the paediatric ward. It was devastating to find yourself with the remnants of children's bodies, you experience their tragedies up close. I remember a girl from the al-Kadry family, her body was completely burned, green and white discharge was leaking from it. All this from a bomb, they were bombing us with new poisons whose nature we don't know. Eight-year-old Bisan had both lower limbs amputated. Once, I sat on her bed to condole with her, but she gave no response apart from asking me to get up because I was sitting on her leg and making it hurt even more. I was terrified. Her leg had been amputated! I felt intense vertigo and my whole body trembled as I looked at her. She repeated her request very politely, 'Auntie, please get off my leg, you're hurting me.' I got up and apologized. I became a nurse and a psychological support. Being there on the children's ward brought me close to them, I began

151

trying to teach the children how to manage with their new, incomplete bodies.

The numbers of dead and wounded children were large, perhaps they formed the greater proportion. It came as one of many surprises how strong they were, how resolute and tough in dealing with everything. I saw this with my own eyes, it was a marvel. Where did they get this courage from? Who taught them this serenity? How did I not see any reactions appropriate to their age – or what is supposedly appropriate. Is it conceivable that they grew old before their time? They had white hair, and they were still children! I would see them lying on their beds, unable to move bodies that had lost limbs, but remaining calm most of the time. I remember that when Ibrahim al-Sawalhy, a boy of 12, learned of his family's death, he just said, 'Alhamdulillah.' Abdel Rahman Radwan was another sole survivor from his family. In the bombing that caught his family home, fifty people were martyred and only he was left. He arrived at the hospital on 12 January, I remember because it was the day we were supposed to discharge Bara. When I heard his story, I rushed to the neighbouring room where they had put him. He was yelling from the pain, his body was burned, his stomach was open and he had a head injury. I brought him a blanket and spent two days caring for him. On the third day, he said to me, 'I want an egg.' God, I was thrilled! I asked the doctor and he said he could eat. There wasn't much food, and we were hungry, but I did have two eggs. It's hard to describe it to you – they were the last eggs we had, and we were so hungry, and my mother said, 'What about your brother?' I said to her, 'But he's a child!' He ate both eggs and when I saw him eating them I smiled for the first time in a long time. Here's what I think: deep down, I was sad and hurting because we would be leaving him that same day. A carer of one of the other patients saw how much I looked after Abdel Rahman and she asked me, 'Is he your relative?' I replied, 'No, he's not.' Abdel Rahman said, 'Of course she is, she's my auntie.' I still think about him, a boy on his own, without a mother or a family.

What astonishes me most is I have kept my sanity despite everything I've seen. I've seen awful things, many people did things I can't speak about – in fact I don't ever want to, I prefer to forget. Perhaps Iman Mussalim's injury is the worst one I saw. She was a plump woman of 33, her brother brought her to the hospital. I remember her and her name because what I witnessed on her I had never seen in my life. Her right hand had a hole in it, a circular hole as though a sharp tool had cut out a piece of her palm. Her legs too. In fact, her whole body was gouged with circles and semicircles. It was so strange. What kind of weapon was this, that acted like a mouse gnawing the sides of a bread roll? With every new war, the Israelis force us to experience new weapons. I nursed her, I helped her brother who was caring for her. We would clean her wounds which were weeping pus, and change her dressings without anaesthetic. Her brother was an enormous man, he insisted on caring for her and sterilizing her wounds himself, and I assisted him. Everyone said she would die within hours, but thanks to our care she lasted three months, until she developed sepsis and she died. Was this a humane action? Would it have been better to let her die quickly without suffering such agony for three months? But could we have let her wounds rot without doing anything? I don't know, I really don't know. She died in the end and had relief from her torments. Like her, my brother Abdullah suffered then died.

Yes! I became a nurse suddenly. I changed dressings, I wiped away pus, I sterilized wounds, moving from

153

wounded patient to wounded patient. This experience brought me closer to the human body in a changed state rather than its normal, familiar state, and in doing so I gained a different perspective. I started to see our exist-ence in a different way – I will never go back to what I was before. I don't know whether this is a good thing or not, all I know is that we will go mad if not for our faith in God.

ABDEL RAHMAN EYAD ABU HAMADA
17 years old
Al-Maghazi Camp

The day of 7 October seemed strange and shocking. We began hearing rockets. I was at home, I had an exam at school. We saw the rockets being fired and took a photo of them, thinking they were like the previous bombing raids we've been used to for years. But we soon learned that Hamas had launched an attack – they called it 'the al-Aqsa Flood' – with the aim of liberating Palestine. But at the time I didn't understand what was happening, I was still in my school clothes. That same day, the Israeli occupation began bombing us directly. They bombed the towers, I saw bombing destroy a whole tower block in front of me on 5 November 2023 in al-Aloul massacre. We had been displaced to dar sidi*, Muhammad al-Haj Ahmed, gathering there together with my mother's brothers and sisters, around twenty people. Life became nothing but the roar of bombs or the struggle to find sleep. It was when I was trying to doze off that they bombed the house with a missile. I tried to keep my family safe. I opened the door and found that the wall and the ceiling were tilted, I saw my family under the destroyed wall, shrapnel was falling on them. I ran to save them. That's when we realized the bomb had fallen on the women's room – my aunts were injured, the ceiling and the wall had collapsed on them. Meanwhile shrapnel landed in all directions and everyone was trapped under the rubble. I saw a little girl, I didn't recognize her, she was about eighteen months old and cut in two. I picked her up and gave her to my sister's husband. All the tower blocks in al-Maghazi were destroyed and people had gone down with them. I

* Dar sidi – my grandfather's house.

was numb, I was looking around and couldn't believing what I was seeing. Over 150 people died that day. All the residents in this neighbourhood were civilians, but they dropped those bombs on us even so. I began to help, gathering up body parts and offering help to the injured, but we couldn't find many of the corpses as they had been buried under the rubble, mixed with metal and stone. When we lost hope of finding them, we concentrated on rescuing the living. Afterwards they announced a ceasefire, so we went home – it was close to another neighbourhood in al-Maghazi where there had been another massacre – and we repaired it, and our large family gathered there again. We finished cleaning and arranging the house, and in the evening of the first day after the ceasefire, at around seven o'clock while we were preparing dinner, they bombed us again. They bombed five houses at the same time – our house, and the houses of the Nuwasara and Abu Rahma families. That bombing on 24 December reaped over 150 additional victims in a new massacre.

I was home at the moment of the explosion. It felt as though the world around me exploded in red. I was blasted into the neighbour's house and only woke up in hospital. At that point, I didn't know what had happened. I had injuries in my head and my feet, my body was full of wounds, fractures and shrapnel. During the explosion, I remember being conscious as the force sent me flying through the air until I slammed into a cement wall, then a metal door fell on me and I couldn't move or get up. I lost my whole family in that bombing. All of them were martyred: my mother and father, my uncles, my grandfather and my grandmother, my aunts and their children. There were about forty-five individuals in the same bombing, and no one survived apart from me. There is no one left from the Abu Hamada family, or from my mother's family, the al-Haj Ahmed family.

My father, Eyad Abu Hamada, worked as a civil servant in the Palestinian Authority, and my mother, Randa al-Haj Ahmed, was a teacher and school principal. All the people around us were civilians, I knew them all – they were good, peaceful people. My older sister, Dana Abu Hamada, and her little daughter Bana also died in the bombing. I was a high-school student studying in the literary stream.* I dreamed of becoming a photographer, but now everything has changed. The following day, my uncle told me that my whole family had died. I couldn't grasp it – why did they bomb us like that? The quantity of missiles was tremendous, as though an explosive barrel landed on us. Our four-storey house was completely destroyed, turned to dust like the other buildings around it. They buried everyone, but they still haven't found my mother even now, it's like she has vanished under the wreckage. And not just my mother – a number of my family members are still there, they can't extract their bodies to bury them.

I stayed in hospital for twenty-two days, and the bombing all around us was relentless. Drones targeted us while we travelled. We turned to Doctors Without Borders for help to move but I saw for myself how they destroyed the road in front of us, even though they knew it was a medical organization. They even fired on us when we were in hospital. We had no food, water or electricity, the place was packed – several families were sheltering there, and the floor was filled with injured people, corpses and displaced people. Everyone was tangled up in each other, it was suffocating. In the middle of this darkness, they

* For the final two years of secondary education, Palestinian students choose a specialization of literary, scientific or various vocational education streams.

recognized the body of my sister's cherished little girl from her clothes. They couldn't find her head. She was a year and a half, I loved her so much.

After days of torture in al-Aqsa Hospital, we moved to Rafah, thinking it would be a safer area, but the bombing carried on there as well. I lived in a tent with my uncle's wife, Khitam Abu Hamada, trying to keep away from the drone bombings. Living in a tent was hell; changing my dressings was a painful process. I was moved in a donkey cart, and once I fell off and my wounds opened up again. I couldn't walk, they had to carry me across the sand in the camp, where there were no facilities and no water. Going to the bathroom was a torturous journey, because the wheelchair couldn't move over sand. We used to rely on a borrowed chair to get me there. Life in a tent lacked even the most basic necessities. The heat was unbearable, flies swarmed everywhere, and in the winter the cold grew so harsh it was almost impossible to endure. My wounds burned, and at night the pain was so intense I couldn't sleep.

The road from the hospital to Rafah was a scene of pure horror. We left by the coast and saw nothing but destruction along the way. The area between Deir al-Balah and Rafah had disappeared completely. Buildings were wiped off the face of the earth, roads were totally destroyed; everything was razed to the ground. It was like entering some strange, unfamiliar world. If I hadn't known al-Rashid Street, I wouldn't have recognized the place – it had become wreckage surrounded by corpses. Corpses couldn't save each other from being stolen, I saw Israelis taking bodies from the area. In October, before I was injured and before the massacre of my family, I used to work as a volunteer. I would help people and hand out food and water. We used to stand in front of the Netzarim checkpoint and the tanks would line up, and I saw them kill a young guy there, right in front of me, just a normal man standing in the middle of the crowd. In the blink of an eye, they shot him and left him there. That happened several times, right in front of me. Doctors were killed, universities destroyed. I couldn't understand why they were targeting education. They have destroyed the University of Palestine and the Faculty of Medicine entirely. They haven't left a trace of academic life behind. My school, the al-Maghazi Prep School for Boys, wasn't safe from the massacres either, it was the victim of a tank artillery bomb. Ten students died straight away, and time after time we would gather the dismembered bodies of the martyrs, my friends and classmates. The school was utterly destroyed.

Despite everything, I want to go back to Gaza, I don't see a life for myself outside it, away from where I lived with my family and my brothers and sisters. I was the youngest, the spoiled baby, surrounded by their love and concern, my father never ignored a request from me. Before 7 October, my life was more like paradise. My sister Dana was a well of my secrets, she was a second mother to me. Her small daughter was a piece of my heart, the first grandchild in the family, seeing her happy made my day. We couldn't sleep without checking she was OK. She was killed by a bomb while she was in her father's arms. My older brother was a stage actor about to get married to a girl he loved, Shahad al-Haj Ahmed, but she died with him, she died in the same house and in the same massacre.

There is no one left from my family, no one left.

WAFAA ASAAD ABU SAMAAN
28 years old
Beit Lahia

I was eight months pregnant when the war began. I lived
with my husband and my two daughters, Maryam and
Shahad. On 7 October, we were at home, I was getting
myself and my daughters ready for school. I asked my
husband to take Shahad with him when he went to work.
But when we heard the rockets and the disturbance, I
realized a war had begun. My husband said it was just
manoeuvres, but I was positive it would be war. We have
been through wars before and so I believed it would
pass like all the others. My husband wanted to leave,
but I stopped him and locked the door and told him he
wasn't going anywhere. We stayed at home, I was horribly
frightened. The screaming and the noise from the rockets was terrifying – clearly, it wasn't manoeuvres. After a
few hours, the Israelis started bombing madly, successive
fire belts rained down from the sky without stopping. We
were living on the top floor. I had shown signs of going
into early labour. The doctor told me I mustn't move or
I might lose the baby. My husband was frightened and
asked me to go to my family home in Jabalia because
the situation had become dangerous. I went and stayed
with my family for ten days, but the bombing there was
very heavy, they destroyed entire housing blocks. I was
a cancer patient as well as being pregnant. Seeing dismembered corpses made me even more terrified. The
bombing was so intense, the window glass went flying and
landed on us. My family home was filled with displaced
people, so my husband decided we would go back to our
home – there was bombing everywhere, and nowhere
was safer than anywhere else. I lost two uncles during the

160

bombardment, Sami and Hany Harb. I was constantly looking at my daughters, 8-year-old Maryam and 5-year-old Shahad, with choking grief and intense fear.

When we returned from my family's house, I no longer slept in our top-floor apartment. I started to sleep in my father-in-law's apartment on the ground floor, with my daughters, my aunt and my husband's sisters. Actually, I couldn't sleep at all from worrying about my husband who was sleeping alone in our apartment. My health got worse because I had stopped receiving my cancer treatment – medicines had stopped arriving in Gaza due to the war. This didn't worry me, all my thoughts were bent solely on the lives of my husband and daughters, and on my baby. My father-in-law was a doctor at Kamal Adwan Hospital and sometimes he would bring me some medicines, but they weren't always enough. We were used to having a suitcase perpetually ready, containing our official documents and my medicines – we Gazans live in constant readiness for any war. I was still in mourning for my uncles, I was very attached to them. From the intensity of grief, I lost the ability to move and I began to feel pain in my belly. I was sobbing incessantly. I suffered a lot before the war, when I came down with cancer. The doctors told me I wouldn't be able to have children again, and even though I had two daughters, I thought of my husband and my girls, and I told him to marry again. But my husband refused, he said girls were like boys as far as he was concerned, and it wasn't important to have a boy. He assured me, 'There's nothing better than girls!' I felt deficient because I hadn't had a son, I was hurting a lot, but a miracle happened and I became pregnant while I was sick. I was so frightened of losing my baby, I was certain he was a boy. At night, I would pray to God to keep him, even if giving birth would put my life in danger. I wanted

161

to make my husband happy. He wasn't just a husband: he was a friend and lover and brother. His name was Saeed Rafat Abu Ful, he worked in tiling. He was over-joyed when he learned of my pregnancy, I'll never forget how his face lit up. None of the family could believe the news. I only wanted him to see his son. My husband got everything ready, he bought everything our expected child would need.

That day, 19 October, I wanted to be with my husband and daughters as a family under a single roof. I was upset we had left him by himself, so I went from my uncle's house on the ground floor to ours. I laid out mattresses for my daughters on the living room floor, next to their father, away from the windows. I had prepared the house and painted the walls and got it ready to welcome the baby. For a moment, I felt very happy, beside my husband and my daughters in my clean house. We sat following the news, and we predicted the areas most likely to be bombed. My husband asked me to go to sleep, but how could we sleep when the bombing was non-stop? He said to me, suddenly, 'Pray and then go to sleep. I have a feeling I'm going to be martyred today. If that happens, I know I'll be leaving a strong woman who will take care of my children.' When he said that, I burst out crying. The first missile fell on us not half an hour later, but it didn't explode. We leapt up and I threw myself on top of the girls to protect them. It was terrifying. My husband got up from the mattress – he wanted to hug us – when the second missile fell and exploded. The whole house col-lapsed on top of us. I was conscious and I saw everything. We went flying, and each of us landed in a different place. I could hear my daughters screaming, and I was shouting, 'Help me! Over here!' I heard my husband's voice recit-ing the shahada, the girls were crying. I saw myself trying my hardest to raise the heavy stones and rocks that had fallen on me and my daughters, the girls were screaming, 'Mama!' All of a sudden, it seemed to me that I could feel a warm liquid, and I heard a newborn screaming. I thought I was losing my baby, and I said to myself, has he died? I really felt the labour pains and I could feel the warmth of my waters but all my thoughts in that moment were to save my girls. I began to dig at the rubble with my fingers to get to them. I heard people's voices nearby and yelled, 'I'm alive! Get my girls!' but my daughter's cries began to get fainter, and I knew they had been rescued thanks to the people's voices. I heard them saying, 'Wafaa and her husband have been martyred,' so I shouted from under the rubble, 'My husband is alive! Help him... help him!' And I heard his voice saying, 'La ilaha illa Allah...'. I heard them saying, 'Bring a stretcher,' and suddenly I shouted, 'Watch out, my leg's cut off!' I had seen how the ceiling had fallen on it. I didn't feel any pain at that point. I could see that a thin piece of skin was all that connected my leg to the rest of my body. I calmly asked them to pick me up, all my thoughts were bent on my baby I thought I had lost. Later on, I realized that the crying I heard and the warm gush of water were just hallucinations. I hadn't lost him as I had thought, but in that moment I was certain I had heard my baby's voice. In the ambulance, I started to feel like I was falling and I lost consciousness. I was trying to touch my severed leg, and the paramedic yelled, 'Sister, don't go to sleep!' When the ambulance moved off, I spent a moment thinking that I was leaving my baby there, under the wreckage. Then I blacked out completely, and I no longer remember exactly what happened after that, but I was certain, in that moment, that I had lost my baby. I started to wonder, 'Where is the umbilical cord?' and other weird things.

I knew that I was going to die, but I *had to* stay alive, even though I had already lost my baby.

I woke up in the Indonesian Hospital fifteen days later, to the voice of my uncle, and I couldn't see anything. My uncles were crying all around me, I could hear voices, then I blacked out again. I didn't know myself for an instant and I asked someone nearby, 'Who am I?' In total, the coma lasted fifteen days. My uncle, Saeed Abu Samaan who worked in al-Shifa Hospital, visited me constantly. He told me that my baby was alive, and showed me a scan. I was shocked, I had been so certain I had left him under the rubble. I couldn't distinguish reality from fantasy. My delusions seemed more real to me than the truth. I would imagine my uncle saying to me, 'I will save your child!' then I would black out again. After I woke from the coma, they moved me to the upper floor where my daughters were. I saw them for the first time after the bombing. I was in one bed, Maryam was in another bed and Shahad was in a third. I saw my daughters and I relaxed a little, despite their injuries. Maryam had burns and shrapnel injuries, she had lost a finger, she had had some deep wounds and a broken pelvis. Shahad's teeth were broken, she had an injury to her eye, her leg was broken and she had significant shrapnel injuries all along her back from her neck to the bottom of her spine. They came and told me that my husband was martyred. Inwardly, I already knew, but I didn't say a word. I just told them, 'I heard him reciting the shahada until his last breath.' Yes, I remembered my husband's voice reciting while we were under the rubble.

I stayed in the Indonesian Hospital for forty-five days. I saw everything. I had procedures without anaesthetic, and because I was pregnant I wasn't allowed to take a lot of medicine. The cancer medication wasn't available either. The doctors were expecting me to die, and honestly I believed it too. Death was inevitably on my mind, and the minds of everyone around me. My hand and my leg were amputated, and the second leg was very damaged. Shrapnel and burns covered my body. I witnessed it all: the siege, the massacres, everything that can't be described. I learned that they bombed my family's neighbourhood and heard stories of the destruction, and meanwhile my daughter Maryam's situation got worse. The bombardment over the hospital never stopped and I was on the second floor, in the trauma ward. Shrapnel and glass rained down on us, while rocks fell from above. I don't remember sleeping, I only remember the hunger and thirst. Every second, I was convinced that my end was near. I couldn't even put my hand on my stomach to feel my baby moving. There were only the medical staff, the patients, the displaced people, the attendants in the hospital. Shrapnel was flying all over the place. With my own eyes I saw children torn to pieces on the ground, even though I couldn't move. I would catch a glimpse of them from the corners of my eyes, I saw every corpse. My family would drop solutions into my mouth, a few drops at a time, to keep me alive. One day, my brother came to tell me that they were taking me with them, they had miraculously survived after our house was bombed. I didn't object, I said, 'Do what you think best.' He put me in a wheelchair, crying all the while, and I looked at him, scared. They moved me to my grandfather's house under bombardment, and even though I survived, my face still bore burn scars. My eyes had been closed, but now I could open them a little. It was a blessing from God that I couldn't see clearly, the corpses and body parts on the road surrounded us in every direction.

We arrived at my grandfather's house under violent bombardment. When we got there, they put me on the bed, and shrapnel and glass kept falling on us as the bombing continued, but incredibly we survived. My sister the nurse and my uncle the doctor cared for me, despite everything. But as the bombing intensified, they had to leave. I asked them to leave me behind and save themselves, and take my daughters with them. It was hard to move me, so I told them, 'This is my fate, leave me and escape.' But they refused and insisted on staying with me, saying, 'We will stay with you, we die or live together.' I begged them to leave me to die, I had reached the stage of being content to die, but they refused and told me that there was a safe corridor we would all leave by. In the end, I was forced to agree to the journey, and they took me south with them. That was the worst day of my life. The road they had said was safe was filled with death and destruction. I saw Israeli soldiers bombing corpses, dogs eating human remains. That was 21 November, and we stayed at the checkpoint from seven in the morning until four in the afternoon. The scene was pure horror: corpses on both sides of the road, cats and dogs walking around with human blood smeared around their mouths, people whose bodies had been torn to pieces and their things scattered all around. That day was rainy, but even so, the bombing never stopped. My brother was pushing me in the wheelchair among the large crowds of people fleeing, whenever we moved I would scream in pain. I wished a bomb would fall on me and end my suffering. With every jolt in the road my horrific agony got worse. The Israeli soldiers were taking young men at the checkpoint and killing them straight away, right in front of us. I saw them murder a man in cold blood. My brother blurted out, 'If they take me or kill me, our cousin will push your wheelchair, have patience.' I was sobbing and reciting the Qur'an, and during the inspection, they asked us to raise our hands. I saw severed hands, and amputees, and I was frightened they would take me too. But I kept reciting the Qur'an out loud.

The Israeli soldiers ordered us to sit on the ground with bowed heads. I was missing limbs and I couldn't move. They yelled at everyone to lower their heads, and I bent my head forward until it touched my stomach, I couldn't get it any lower. People all around me were forced into the mud, we were all humiliated, and still they screamed at us, saying: *You Gazans, you dogs. Get your heads down, you animals. You all deserve to die. You, woman, get your head down, you terrorist.* We were just children, women, pregnant women and old people. We stayed like that for three hours, and all the while they were screaming: *Go left, Go right.* We would walk a little way then they would close the road, and if one of you dropped something, you couldn't pick it up, they would shoot you if you did. They were shooting at random. I was scared they would murder me and shoot me in the belly – they had shot a pregnant woman at ten o'clock that morning. I was terrified and began to hide my belly, putting a bag in front of it to hide my pregnancy. Everyone asked me to hide it. I had already seen a pregnant woman they had shot in the belly, in al-Awda Hospital. The soldiers fired at my cousin when he put his things on the ground, trying to help my brother. They shot at his feet and yelled: *Walk, or I shoot you.* My cousin froze, it was a wonder he survived, I was screaming and crying, asking him to hurry up. We walked a little way then they ordered us to stop. They spoke to us from behind a sandbank. They didn't face us directly, they were hiding behind that mound, and they spoke in Arabic through microphones. We were surrounded by tanks and cameras.

After that, my brothers picked me up in my wheelchair

and they put it on a donkey cart to take me to my aunt, she was a nurse living in Nuseirat. They secured me tightly on the cart as the roads weren't paved, and the cart jolted with every step. I began screaming in indescribable agony as if I was being slaughtered a thousand times over with every shake. My wounds were splitting open and bleeding, I screamed until we reached Nuseirat, broken and exhausted; I almost passed out. They put me on a mattress on the ground. We had no food or drink, my blood pressure was very low. Then we moved from Nuseirat to Rafah, to our relatives' house. My temperature rose and there was a terrible pain in my belly, so they took me to the European Hospital. My injuries were infected and they changed my dressings. After two weeks I started to go into labour. They told me that a natural birth was impossible and I had to have a caesarean because my body was riddled with shrapnel and my remaining leg had no flesh – it was paralysed, so it was as if I had no legs at all. During labour they transferred me to Nasser Hospital in Khan Younis, to the maternity ward. The road was full of holes, the khabat* and the bombardment had become second nature by that point. When we reached the hospital, they were surprised to learn that I was a cancer patient and I had to have an additional medicine, so I waited for my father and my brother to return from a laboratory in Khan Younis. I continued having contractions. When my father returned four hours later, the doctors said the birth might be impossible. They were forced to choose between my life and the baby's.

The doctor told my father, 'You have to choose between her life and the life of the baby.' My father replied, 'I don't want to lose her!' My father loved me very much, I was his spoiled darling. 'I choose my daughter,' he said. I said, 'I

* Khabat is a Gazan word for the noise of bombardment.

don't want to lose my son, I choose my son!'

The doctor was marvellous. I don't remember his name now, but I know that later they bombed him and his wife and children, and they all died. Back then, this doctor tried to convince me that I was gambling with the lives of myself and my son. He was as kind and tender as a father. And then I don't know what happened, but suddenly the labour pains vanished, my waters hadn't broken yet, my womb just completely shut down. The doctors were bewildered, and after that I went a whole week without giving birth. In that critical period, when they thought my case was hopeless, they decided to transfer me to Egypt. That day, the news came that my name was recorded on the list of wounded.* That day felt like a year. All I wanted was to save my son. I was desperate, because even if I was able to give birth, there was no milk, no nappies or food, and I couldn't nurse him because of the cancer and the aggressive infections from my wounds.

I passed the Rafah crossing and they transferred me from the Palestinian ambulance to the Egyptian ambulance. The pain was non-stop. The paramedic asked me, 'Are you pregnant?' And I replied, 'Yes, this is the last day of the ninth month.' Pain was attacking my body from everywhere, labour pains mixed with pain from my injuries – I wasn't even aware I was giving birth! I was screaming in pain, thinking it was only the pain from the wounds. When we arrived at Arish Hospital, the paramedic said to me, 'You're in labour, you're giving birth.' And I replied, 'No, it's just my injuries.' It felt as though every cell of my body was being sliced up with knives. And in half an hour, my son was born. He had survived. I called him Refat. I gave birth on 4 December.

* This refers to the list of injured people accepted for medical evacuation.

After Refat was born, my uncle Dr Abu Samaan was martyred in Jabalia. He was like my father, full of tenderness and chivalry. Refat came, and my beloved uncle left. Now, my daughter is still living in a tent, and she has nothing to eat. She is injured. I used to live with my children, my daughter is supposed to be at school, but now she is hungry and there are no medicines for her, not even any clean water to drink, she is sick. I am so afraid I will lose her. I don't know what to tell you and what to leave out. A hundred people from our family were killed in a single bombing. I was in hospital when I heard the news, drifting in and out of consciousness, but I could hear them speaking. A sniper shot my cousin. My father-in-law, my uncle, my husband were all martyred. Even my aunt Ghada didn't survive. There isn't a lot of my family left.

After Refat was born, a new string of surgeries began on my shredded, dismembered body. I still remember them saying to my mother, 'Let her die in peace.' They didn't believe I would live, but I did and so did my son. Please, Samar, tell all of this! I survived, but my heart is dead. Say that after the Baptist massacre, when my husband saw children torn to pieces and the body parts of his friends, he hoped to die, he wanted to die, he was content with his fate – he couldn't bear this life.

ISRA MUHANNA
33 years old
Al-Zahra

What was I doing on 7 October?

I was trying to wake my kids when we heard the missiles.

At first, we thought they were the usual Israeli missiles, a strike or two or three and it would be over, as happened from time to time. But we soon discovered these rockets were coming from here, from Gaza. We thought that perhaps they were a response to a new Israeli bombing, as Israel would usually target people it had an eye on. Honestly, we kept away from politics. We have lived under a stifling siege for years, and because of this, bewilderment has reigned. For years we have felt like prisoners in Gaza, at the mercy of their raids – so what could they possibly be doing now?

I have three children, as beautiful as the moon. In the past, the town of al-Zahra was close to the Netzarim settlement, and it was a well-organized, attractive city, full of residential tower blocks. The bombing operations began targeting the city five days later, they started bombing the tall towers, I used to live in one of them. They started destroying the northern towers, then Karama Towers. At first the Israelis would call and threaten us: *Leave your homes, we are going to bomb you.* But after a while they stopped giving warnings, they started bombing the tower blocks over the heads of their residents without any warning at all, the warnings were just in the early days. I was with my husband and children, we could hear people screaming and the bombs booming. I was terrified for my children but we decided to wait – no one wants to leave their home and wander towards the unknown. But after a few days, the Israelis called in the middle of the night: *You must clear the towers and leave at once. Get out and head to the sea. Go!* We had no choice. We left immediately.

As soon as we left our building and headed towards the sea, the towers started collapsing one after another. They were smashing the tower blocks like they were cardboard boxes. High-rise buildings turned to dust in a matter of seconds – it was like a scene from the apocalypse. We were going far away, leaving our homes behind us. They kept bombing, violently and vengefully. The tower blocks fell one after another, even though they knew that al-Zahra didn't contain any resistance and all its residents were civilian employees, they were no threat to anyone.

We went to my family's neighbourhood in the south of the Strip, al-Zawayda, which was considered the safest area in previous wars. The movement of displacement from north to south was considerable, and the houses there filled up with displaced people fleeing the bombing. People opened their homes for people escaping death, even to people they had never met before, all were helping each other. We thought it would only last for a few days, then things would go back to how they were before. Then before long, the bombardment took aim at al-Zawayda, which the Israeli army had claimed was safe. They bombed the Hassouna family home – our neighbours, who we were close to – on the pretext that some of the young men of the family were with the resistance, so the Israelis alleged. The Hassouna house was full of civilians and displaced people, they had celebrated their daughter's engagement the previous day. I was in my family home when the strike took place. We knew, from the force of the explosion, that it was serious. We had begun to have some experience of death – all we needed was to hear the sound of the missile and we already knew the extent of death and destruction it would leave behind. We rushed to the street to seek out survivors, and found the remaining family members searching under the rubble for the rest. Aya Hassouna, the girl who had got engaged just one day earlier – her father was looking for her, hoping she had survived and perhaps she had come to visit us, but she was buried beneath the wreckage along with her cousins who had been displaced to their house. The ceiling collapsed on them, and they all died. Most of the people who attended her engagement party had been buried under the rubble with her. Some neighbours were trying to move the debris but the Israeli plane wouldn't let them finish, they were bombed and killed as well. The same tragedy has been repeated in many cases.

That was the way of things: whoever died was dead, and whoever survived was left to their torment. Despite our misery as we waited our turn to die, my family and I never stopped condoling with our neighbours, even though the random bombings had no mercy for anyone. In the first two months, our sufferings began to worsen because of the lack of food and drink. And it didn't stop there – we began to lose everything. We could no longer even reach the wounded or help people, because drones would bomb the first responders without mercy. We used to cook for the injured and take food to them, my family and I would go by car to distribute food and clothing, we would dodge the bombing and try to reach out a helping hand to others.

I studied nursing, but I never worked because I had been absorbed in caring for my children. With the beginning of the war, I was constantly providing aid to the injured people around me. It was strange to find myself always running to provide treatment, as if Gaza had become a city only of dead and wounded. Once, after a bombing, I came across a young girl who had lost all her family. She had a pelvic fracture and couldn't move. I carried her to my family's house, and she was in intense pain as there were no painkillers. There had come to be a spirit of cooperation among everyone, despite everything we were going through. I worked as a nurse for others as much as I could, but even so I wasn't satisfied. Once, they wanted to know whether a little girl brought out from under the rubble was still alive. She wasn't more than a year and a half, completely cold. I knew she had died some time before. The truth is, many people died under the rubble, mostly from suffocation because help was too late in arriving. There were no medicines, no first responders, no ambulances, and any that were available were targeted by Israeli drones, which slowed down the rescue operations. As the bombardment continued without stopping, people were left under the wreckage for days. The case of that little girl was similar to what happened with our neighbours from the Hassouna and the Saidam families, where the diggers didn't come in time. My brothers went down to help dig out the neighbours from under the debris, but they couldn't keep going; their faces were white from the horror of the situation. We would barely have finished taking people out from the rubble before the bombing moved somewhere else, so we would run from place to place without a break. Many people died, more than you can imagine. Even our neighbours, the Aalyouma family, were bombed and killed. They were decent people with no connection to politics, or to Hamas or the resistance. They were humble, respectable people, but they weren't spared.

I saw the corpse of a young man go flying in front of me in a nearby bombing. His father was looking for him, then his brother found him and carried his body in his arms. I was walking in between bodies, I saw them one after another. There was a group of women in front of me, injured and wounded, and I rushed towards them despite being afraid – I knew the Israelis resumed bombing if they saw first responders. I was heading towards the wounded women next to the destroyed house when I passed the young man whose body I had seen flying through the air. I didn't go to him because, quite simply, I knew he was dead, and he didn't need me. I said to myself, I must keep my remaining strength for the living. Fear went with me, but I kept going. Strength of heart comes to some and not others, it has no connection to courage or cowardice, it's something that can't be explained. It's not easy, seeing human limbs and other things I can't speak about. My siblings and I would run to aid people. We were one of those families that possesses a heart capable of bearing such things. My mother was frightened for us because of the repeat explosions after a bombing, and she would shout, calling after us in the street, but she couldn't stop us. We couldn't let people die, that was never a choice. They were our neighbours, our loved ones, our dear friends. We couldn't wait for the Civil Defence teams to arrive, we would run to them, neighbours and displaced people who sought refuge with us.

We were living with some displaced people who we had welcomed into our building. None of us had any relationship with the resistance or with Hamas. They were lying when they said they were targeting Hamas – they bombed us and they knew we were just civilians. We didn't think they would resume bombing after having destroyed the buildings around us. We were occupied with caring for the displaced; we had pregnant women, others who had had caesarean births. For pregnant women on the verge of giving birth, it was extremely hard. I

175

was stitching up wounds, removing stitches, caring for the children and women in appalling circumstances I can't talk about in detail. There were no phone lines, the bombing never stopped, and all while the medical cadre was busy with the injured.

When you are preoccupied with the injuries of others, your own takes you by surprise. On the night of 10 October, all of a sudden, I woke up and felt as though someone was pushing me outside. When a bomb lands on you, you feel nothing, you hear nothing. I was in one room with my husband, my children, and my 65-year-old father-in-law. Every night, I would open my eyes and see him praying the dawn prayer. He would get up to perform his wudu', and I would wait until he had finished before I performed mine. That day, seconds before the strike, I opened my eyes and asked myself, has he finished his wudu' or not? And after that I no longer remember anything. It's strange, as if it was a dream, or a nightmare.

I woke up and my eyes were full of gunpowder, I found it hard to breathe, as if I was choking. I couldn't open my eyes, I didn't know what had happened. I thought I was dreaming and would be getting up to pray, and when they tried to pull me out, I screamed with pain. My shoulder was broken but my screaming meant I was still alive, and the people around me were relieved. Whoever it was that tried to save me couldn't see very well, black dust hung heavy and darkness smothered everything. I couldn't make out the bodies, sometimes they were black, at other times disfigured. One of them asked me, 'Was there anyone next to you?' That's when I remembered my children. They hadn't been next to me, the explosion had blasted them far away. They brought me out of the wreckage then they found my children. I learned that my brothers and sisters were woken by the shaking, and the upper floors where the displaced people were living weren't that damaged. My family told me that they tried to come downstairs to check on us, but they couldn't – everything on the lower floors was destroyed, and debris covered every corner. I remembered my father-in-law had been asleep in bed when the explosion hit. The explosion blasted his mattress with him, he slammed into the wall and died. The displaced people still under the rubble were unconscious. My brother told me it was like Judgement Day, and I was calling out when I was under the wreckage.

My mother told me she couldn't see anything, she only heard my brother's voice when he was shouting. She said that they turned on the torches on their phones to see, then they saw my mother wandering around, she didn't know where she was or what had happened. At that moment they were pulling me out from under the rubble, and they found my daughter, who in turn found her little sister. The trauma my family suffered was profound. After the house shook, the windows smashed and the children were sent flying from place to place. It was a horrifying shock for them, suddenly realizing that they were the ones being bombed. My father, they told me later, just stood there dumbfounded. It was like a nightmare that simply can't be believed, ruin and destruction everywhere, as if we were in a terrifying dream. My young daughter who was 2 years old, she had her head split open. As for me, I had a fractured neck, shoulder and ribs, with burns to my back and body. My daughter Bisan, who was 10 years old, took her little sister out from under the debris. She was crying from pain, her head was bleeding, while my brothers stood there powerless. They who had saved everyone else, they couldn't save my little daughter! My other daughter told me I was screaming and shaking from cold while she held her sister, unable to do anything. No one could get near me because the ground was hot as fire because of the missile. So my brothers stood there powerless, and my daughter Bisan stood holding her little sister and looking at her exposed skull. My husband told me later than he woke from the blast and felt himself flying through the air. He found himself lying, thrown on the ground, and thought it was a dream until he heard my brothers saying, 'Come on, wrap Isra in a blanket,' and he thought I was dead. He told me, 'When I heard that, I got to my feet.' My brothers told me they suddenly saw a man covered with dust, with red eyes and eyebrows painted with white dust, coming up to them like a strange wild beast, saying stupidly, 'What's wrong with Isra?' and it was only then that they realized it was my husband. His rib was broken by the blast, which was so violent that bodies went flying and were broken. All our bodies were broken. I still have scars from the burns. They told me that I spoke in the ambulance, asking if it was a dream and asking about my children, but I don't remember any of it. They took me to hospital in the end, my husband followed us while I was unconscious.

The pain was strange, I couldn't understand it. My family couldn't come near me at first. They were traumatized, even though they had saved the neighbours before, but when one of your own is injured, it becomes hard to move. I was a nurse, I saw what suffering meant, and I have lived through death and war. We in Gaza know war, I am a daughter of war. Since birth, we Gazans know what war is. I have strength and faith to bear hardships, and I know my own power, but despite all that, I had never seen what I saw after 7 October. That was something beyond bearing. The Israelis would tell us we don't deserve to live, they want to turn us to dust, all of us without discrimination. But I stood my ground stubbornly, I wanted to live. I said to the nurse in hospital, 'I can't breathe, I can't.' I asked for oxygen, I had swallowed a lot of gunpowder and I couldn't breathe, I was almost dying. Everyone thought I would die, but I was sure that if I vomited up the gunpowder that came out of my guts with the blood, I would be cured. So I threw up black gunpowder, and I saw awful things coming out of my insides. I don't know what poisons they bombed us with, but I was determined to live and I threw all of them up. I kept vomiting until I vomited blood, and after that I started to get better. I was unconscious, I saw strange phantoms and nightmares, then I woke up a little, and blacked out again. I didn't know, at that point, that my father-in-law had died, that my two-year-old daughter was in a critical state and had lost part of her skull. I didn't know because I could hardly hear anything of my surroundings – just calling sounds, as if they were coming from far away.

I don't know how death overlaps with life but I remember that when I saw my daughter after they had stitched her forehead, I realized something very serious had happened to her. Her face was swollen and bloated like an astronaut, her head was entirely wrapped in gauze. At that point we were in al-Aqsa Hospital, and her face was frightening. I was a nurse and I realized my daughter's case was dangerous, her face was blue and swollen, her eyes were swollen and bulging. She was just a child of 2, and her face scared me. I wanted to speak, to move, but I couldn't. The injured kept arriving in droves because the bombing never stopped, and I was afraid. Finally, I saw a nurse and a doctor, and they told me they had decided to operate on my daughter. I felt a little calmer, even though I couldn't speak. My daughter's treatment would take time, they said. Her case was challenging and delicate, involving a number of surgeries that demanded both time and patience. The hospital was filled with injured people, but it also turned into a place for the displaced. They were eating and drinking and living, women and men and children, in the corridors.

I was born in 1990 and have lived through the siege in Gaza. I have witnessed wars and had horrible experiences, but there has been nothing like this. I thought I was used to war and bombardment and cruelty, but not in this way. When the first war happened, I was in university and it was the first time I understood what bombardment means. They struck Hamas military locations, and it was like an earthquake. That was in 2008, and it was only afterwards that we realized what was happening. In 2012 and 2014, the war was during Ramadan and my children were very young. I was living with my husband's family, and the bombing was less savage and there was no displacement. Wars came and some people died, then the wars passed. We relaxed for a time, and then the bombing would start up again. We didn't face anything like what's happening now, this is unprecedented barbarity.

I was thinking of my young daughter's head, her broken skull, and how a small head can be missing a piece and yet she goes on living despite everything. I felt on the edge of a breakdown, but I didn't lose hope. My daughter stayed in hospital for a month receiving intravenous treatments, but her wounds became infected from the poisoned gunpowder in the missiles. The doctors told me that the bombs contained new, lethal chemicals, and the injuries couldn't be healed using traditional antibiotics.

My state of health was extremely bad, and I couldn't move, not even my head. As for my daughter, her condition deteriorated and I could only see her once every five days. I would see her swollen face and bulging eyes, fully

180

aware of how serious her condition was.

When I fully grasped that I had survived, I couldn't believe it. I can't believe I'm still alive. I said to myself, 'I will keep my children alive, my daughter will survive.' That was part of the collective pain we all experienced. There were others who suffered more than me. The genocide I saw has made me grateful for the divine strength that gave me life and meant I could endure. We used to gather firewood so we could cook. At first there was a little gas remaining, but when the gas ran out, we were forced to light fires. We burned all the cardboard we could find, but war kept going for six months.* The house filled with displaced people, and the weather was cold and we needed to light a fire in order to bathe. We suffered greatly. We roamed the streets gathering fuel, my brothers would go far away to gather anything that would burn. When they bombed our house, all our furniture was beneath the wreckage, and we ended up being delighted because we could use the ruins of our house to light a fire! For the moment, life seemed futile. We were regressing to an unfamiliar world, a world of primitive people. We fed the last remnants of our home to the fire, and everyone was doing the same. We were hungry, and there was continual bombing, and the food ran out. When there was any, it was such poor quality it made us ill. What hurt most was seeing the children hungry, they would ask for food and we couldn't give them any. The Israelis controlled al-Zahra where our home was. Now we don't have a home, and I don't know how I will go back. Sometimes I think of my mother, who raised her brother's orphaned son after his father was martyred. I lived with my mother's grief, and we lived with death. We live in perpetual mourning,

* As noted in the preface, the testimonies were collected between March and June 2024.

we don't know joy. We have been in a state of war for a long time. My mother is a child of war. We are the heirs of grief, the heirs of wars. We, the bearers of this legacy, are the ones being annihilated. I look at my daughter, whose skull is fractured because of the Israelis – it is insanity! I don't ask much of life. My mother inherited pain from her mother. I have inherited it from her, and I will pass it on to my daughters. We have inherited war and pain and oppression over the decades, and now we are living through genocide.

SUJOUD ABU HALIB
19 years old
Khan Younis

We know war, we know it very well. In one of these wars, they bombed our house and my father was martyred. That was in 2014. So when I saw rockets leaving Gaza, I knew things would be terrible.

I live with my mother, my three brothers and my brother's wife. My mother is employed in agricultural management and my father worked at the airport. When the Israeli bombing started, we went to Beit Lahia in the north, the opposite way to everyone else and against what the Israelis wanted. Our experience of previous wars made us think they would enter from the south. We stayed in Huboub Street in Beit Lahia for four nights. Those were very difficult nights.

The bombing carried on all the time, buildings were collapsing around us. We moved to the central region. The bombing didn't stop. I said to my family, 'Let's go home, all of Gaza is unsafe.' And my family and I left. As soon as we did, a bomb fell on the house we had been in.

In al-Qarara, as soon as we got back to our house, the Israelis called and ordered us to leave the area. Basically, they were chasing people from one place to another. They told us: *Go, get out!*

At dawn, while we were praying, they rained fire belts on us. And us – what did we do? We were waiting, praying and waiting to die. Just to die! The fire belts never stopped, neither did the death. I don't want to go into the details.

We made it to November. Nothing changed. Constant death, constant bombing, waiting to die. Every morning, I would go out to see the destruction, the shrapnel, the

183

bodies. Then we went to a school with other displaced people, in the Amal neighbourhood. They called it Amal School! Ridiculous, these names.* We had left with what we had on, we didn't take any clothes with us. The Israelis also bombed us at the school for displaced people. My brother was 15 years old, just a kid playing in front of school. The missile ate his body, the shrapnel consumed his body. He didn't die. They saw him moving, so a zannana tried to kill him.

A zannana! Why would it kill a kid? Then they said my cousin Hamza had been martyred. They took my brother to Nasser Hospital. His injuries were critical, very severe. We went to my uncle's house for my little cousin's wake. He was 6 years old.

The Israelis got closer to the school, the screaming and wailing of displaced people announced that danger was approaching. The Israeli army were storming the place. They besieged the school while we were inside. We were terrified. What do the Israelis want from us? They drove us out of our homes and bombed them, then they chased us and bombed us, then they came at us again! They followed us to this school of displaced people. Most of us were women and children. What do they want? They demanded the evacuation of the school, and ordered us to head south.

We didn't know where we were going to go. They were hunting us from place to place. We had been in the school for a month. There were no cars and no petrol. We didn't know what we were going to do. That's how we left, we picked up our bags and walked from al-Tina Street. My middle brother was searching for a means of transport. We walked through gunfire, bullets going in between us

* In Arabic, amal means hope. The construction of the name translates as 'The School of Hope'.

and around us as we walked. That is how the roles were divided – we went out of the school, while they were shooting at our feet and over our heads.

In a nearby school we saw a lot of corpses. Tanks were circling us, separating us, watching us breathe, even. Tanks, soldiers, zannanat. We were waiting for my brother who was late, it seemed he was trapped among the tanks. The drones were all around us, my uncle's disabled wife was with us, and that is how we slowly went forward.

We went without my brother, who had instructed us that if something happened and he was late coming back with transport, then we should carry on and leave him behind. Lines of displaced people were walking all around us, while zannanat, tanks and soldiers moved through the crowd. At one point, I thought they were going to round us up and carry out a mass execution.

We stayed where they left us. It was very, very cold, and we slept on the ground. We had lost my brother. I thought he was dead. But he was searching for us, and we were searching for him.

We reached al-Mawasy Khan Younis, set up a tent and sat inside it with my uncle's family. The tent became our new home.

I used to be afraid of the fire belts, but because of all the death and body parts, I'd grown indifferent. In the hospitals when I was visiting my aunt, I saw terrible things, and I was numb. I think I can't feel anything any more. I think I have stopped feeling. The biggest lie the Israelis told was that they were bombing Hamas. They were bombing us – civilians – women and children.

They killed another cousin of mine with a zannana. I knew him! He wasn't part of Hamas, he had nothing to do with politics. Why did they kill him? They have made people poor. Prices are high and there is no food. A few tins arrive once a week from UNRWA.

My tears have dried up. I'm 19 but I feel like an old woman. When they bombed the school next to us, I saw the displaced people in there, gathering up each other's body parts. After all that, what was the point? They died! They were carrying the wounded and the body parts and wailing around with them. We were hungry, and there was no medicine. There was nothing. We were just dying. They besieged Nasser Hospital. All those people, right in front of me...

Before the war, I told my mother about a dream I had that a fire was following us. There was al-Bahr Street, and I had a vision of ruin. I said to my mother, 'Let's go abroad, let's emigrate, get out of Gaza. Let's leave and go far away.' But my mother said, 'No, we will stay here.' We stayed and my dream became reality. The fire consumed us.

I lived as an orphan, without a father. The Israelis killed him. My father was bathing, they bombed a building next to us and a piece of shrapnel hit him in the head, he bled out and died. I was 9.

What does all this mean? What are they doing to us? There are no words.

We live alongside war drones. They drop down between us, going back and forth. The Israelis don't need to be here in body to kill us. Their advanced weapons and their drones are enough. They don't put a weapon down unless they've used it. Their tanks appear from nowhere and take aim at us.

Once, they shot at my brother. Why? He was running. They just shot at someone who was running. Lots of people have died that way.

Can I say something? I don't have any feelings left, none at all. I just observe all this death, without any emotion. Once, my brother and I were in the street and suddenly a fire belt exploded right beside us. We were so close to the explosions, and what happened? I just stood there in silence. I wasn't frightened, I didn't do anything. Sometimes I think I am dead. I'm always thinking of my brothers, living in tents, in danger of death.

Let's stop here. I don't want to go on.

MUHANNAD RADWAN
15 years old
North Gaza

Samar, can you believe I'm still a kid? I was going to tell you I'm not 15 at all, no one believes it, I'm also surprised when I remember my age, but I decided to be honest.

What's happened since 7 October? Everything that can be imagined, and everything that can't be imagined has happened as well. We were at home that morning, like everyone else. And, like everyone else, we heard the sound of rockets. You must have heard the same details several times, I won't repeat them. Two days later, we got a call from the Israeli army when we were asleep, it was midnight when they told us to leave our house. I was still yawning when my family pushed me outside. We didn't have anywhere to go. I wasn't thinking, there wasn't really time to think of anything but escaping. I didn't say a word and I didn't try to pick anything up when we left. The bombing was crazy, missiles were flying all around us, random missiles looking for targets. One of them hit my aunt's house, Dr Raja Radwan. No ambulances came and I don't even know if there were any, because of those random missiles. It was chaos, missiles were taking aim at anything that moved, the bombing didn't give people a chance to do anything. Even so, my father and my uncles went to my aunt's house, without equipment or anything, they were risking their lives because they knew that anyone going near a bombsite might be bombed themselves. But they went anyway, they were hoping to save any of the living they could, and perhaps take some of the wounded to hospital. And when they got there – what we had expected to happen, happened. The Israelis bombed the house again. The drones had been waiting for people to come and help the wounded in order to bomb them as well. My father was seriously injured, my aunt and her five children were injured, my aunt's husband died. They took my father to hospital. I, my uncles, my wounded aunt and two of her children were forced to flee to Nuseirat Camp in the middle of the Strip. The occupation claimed that the camp was safe but it absolutely wasn't, because the bombing followed us there. There was no safe place in Gaza, everywhere was dangerous. We became displaced in the hope of staying alive, taking our wounded with us and leaving the martyrs behind. My aunt's sons who were seriously injured stayed in al-Shifa Hospital. It wasn't just us, most families had been torn apart, separated into wounded and martyrs.

Days passed like this. Do you want more details? You must have heard them over and over. Each of our stories is just like anyone else's. We were displaced from one place to another, we lost each other with every displacement, we couldn't reach our relatives, we didn't hear much news of them. We became homeless without any refuge, and wounded without care. The hospitals couldn't accommodate the bomb casualties, there were injured people and corpses everywhere, food was more or less non-existent, we were hungry and there was no water to drink apart from a little bit of contaminated water, just so we could go on living. The internet was cut off, and so were the phone networks and the electricity. I felt like I was living in a desert. The only certain, consistent thing – the thing that remained constant and never stopped – was the bombing. I kept silent the whole time, and I did my best not to have any reaction that might make things worse. We were going into the unknown.

On 27 October, my aunt Raja learned that her wounded sons had left al-Shifa Hospital and gone to her sister

Fadwa's house, so she decided to return there to be by their side and care for them. She insisted on it; she couldn't remain away from them. That was two days before the expected ceasefire. The grown-ups said we needed the ceasefire so we could remove the bodies from the rubble, at the very least. Then what happened? They bombed my aunt Fadwa's house, and most of the people inside died, including my aunt Raja. She didn't get to enjoy seeing her children. She went to be at their side, and they died and she died with them. My aunt Fadwa suffered serious burns and fractures in every part of her body. I saw how my family was disappearing, I was watching and waiting for my turn.

The family vanished one after another, and even now I'm in a state of numb shock. I'll go back over events again, I want to understand what happened. Why did we leave our house when the occupation army ordered us to? People were bewildered when the occupation called them and ordered them to leave their homes. Some thought it was nothing but psychological warfare and just a means of forcing people out, because in the end the bombing would reach everyone indiscriminately, warning or not, it was all just pretend. My aunt, they bombed the building next to her without any warning and everyone inside died. In the end, my family decided to leave. As I told you, I woke up and found myself running in the middle of the night towards dar sidi, the bombing was right overhead, explosions surrounded us, I could hear everyone around me preparing themselves to die and muttering verses from the Qur'an while they were running. It felt like we were in a film, like we were just moving targets, waiting to be eliminated. My family was at a loss for what we should do after that, we were trying to go back near to our home but we couldn't because of the bombardment, and two days later, as I told you, they bombed my aunt Raja's house. How did we know? There were no phone calls or electricity, but suddenly my aunt was there with us, bleeding and with torn clothes. I remember it vividly. She had come in that state to tell us what happened, she crawled out from the wreckage and walked all night, alone, all that way, while she was bleeding. She wanted us to go and save her injured sons, the sons who would go into hospital then to their aunt's house and she joined them, only for them all to die together.

We headed south. There is something so ugly about displacement. We became just things that moved, we didn't have clothes or food or anything. In Nuseirat Camp, where we were displaced to, we were extremely thirsty, there was no water, we drank salt water and dirty water. We were prepared to drink anything to keep living. There was no food either. Emaciation and weakness turned me into a different person. I forgot I was just a 15-year-old boy, and I wasn't really the man I felt I was inside. I felt I had grown up, and was capable of things that other kids weren't. I could depend on myself and my family could depend on me – but all these feelings would quickly disappear in the face of hunger, I would shrivel up and go back to being weak. It was freezing, there was no heater, we didn't have any clothes, and wounded and hungry displaced people were distributed across every house.

The Israelis ordered us south, then they chased us. They bombed us again in the house we were displaced to, thirty-three people from our family were martyred all at once. Most of them were babies, just months old. I saw it myself. I was in the heart of the blast and I survived, but the babies didn't, their bodies were so small and fragile. My grandfather died as well – Dr Abdel Raouf Radwan – but not from the bombing, he died because his wound became infected and there was no medical stuff to treat it. It wasn't a serious wound, but the bacteria killed him. There was no medicine or space in the hospitals to care for him. The bombing caught my brother Muhammad, he had terrible injuries to his head and body. It happened while he was looking for food in the streets of the camp. We were at a complete loss, we didn't know where to go and they were hunting us from place to place.

When I heard the news that our house had burned down, I was devastated. I don't know why I felt, for the first time, I was alone. Everything in the house was gone, my whole world, my memories, my things, my papers. I thought of the paintings I had made and kept. Yes, I was an optimistic kid and I used to paint. I was a hard-working student too. I particularly loved maths, it was fun for me. I took part in maths competitions and they chose me to represent Palestine in international competitions. I was sad, really sad. Not because I was a refugee in a tent, but because my life had burned down, all my books and paintings and papers.

We were displaced seven times after that. We left Nuseirat Camp just like all the previous places. The Israelis said they would attack overland on top of the bombing, so we were forced to move on. With every displacement, we thought it was the end. Months passed like years. Every displacement was a life in itself. After Nuseirat, we headed to Rafah. In Rafah we didn't know where to go, and we weren't the only ones. Along with some other displaced people, we managed to find a room and we all piled inside, just lucky to have a ceiling to protect us. There was nowhere in the room to put my feet, most of the people in there with us were sick, there was no care or medicine, none of us had any food, or water, or gas. We were like animals locked in a cage, waiting to die, by whatever means. Not just from bombing, but from starvation, thirst and cold. I remember the taste of thirst was very harsh, much worse than the taste of hunger.

When we realized we couldn't stay like that, piled on top of each other, we decided to leave and look for somewhere else. We couldn't stay, we had no money and rents had shot up because of the war, but we managed to find a small room with a bathroom. Our money began to run out, everything was so expensive. I was surprised how prices went up like that when everyone was poor and had no money. People were forced to pay, and so were we – we had no choice. We were forced to buy cheap things at expensive prices. Then winter came and we needed clothes. We were still wearing the same clothes we had left our house in, they were very light and our bodies were shivering from cold.

Life in Rafah was an unbearable hell. Displacement brought new hardships every day, life was different, full of difficulties and injustice. We were desperately short of water. They put in water pipelines from Egypt, but they were repeatedly cut off. Even when a little water did arrive, it was hard to go out and get it. At night, things were no better, as the noise of the zannanat was loud and terrifying. We felt like prisoners in a place we would only leave to face death. Every trip outside represented a possibility of dying. And with the crazy rise in food prices, we couldn't find sugar or flour any more, and they were fundamental to keeping us alive. Sewage was running in the streets, and there was no one to fix anything! Filth and human waste were gushing in sewage ditches, and disease was widespread. Many people came down with stomach bugs, including us. The most painful thing of all was what began happening between people. Violence grew to be a daily fact. Kind, polite people didn't get anything. People started to get what they needed only through violence and fighting – thugs were the ones who came out on top, they were the ones who got what they wanted. If you were polite, you wouldn't get anything. People were frustrated, hungry, broken; fights broke out just for a drink of water. I was ashamed of myself, waiting in long queues for aid and most of the time coming away with nothing, because I couldn't fight anyone.

I don't want anyone on earth to go through my experience of displacement. I think of my family, half of them we've lost. I think of my aunts and my relatives. I have frightening thoughts while I wait all day to get a dribble of water to wash our hands in, and then I go back to thinking about a fire to cook the tinned food – if we've managed to get hold of some, that is. We anxiously pay attention to know when they announce the distribution of sugar and rice, we wait and wait in lines for hours. How humiliating. Transport has become expensive and usually isn't available, now it mostly relies on donkeys and horses. Our psychological state is bad. I know that I'm not OK, and neither is my family or anyone else, but we shouldn't say so. Why? Because it's considered shameful! But I am not OK, I'm miserable. I think about my school, I think about the large painting I made and hung in my room – it burned down with the house, of course. I think about my pens and notebooks and the things I wrote, my paints and paintbrushes. I imagine it – I wonder how my paintbrushes burned? I don't know why I keep going back over the same words. I feel like a sick person, now. I now have a stomach ulcer that bleeds all the time because of the contaminated water and the tinned food. I started treatment three months ago but the bleeding is still going on in my digestive system, and there's not enough medical services. Weakness creeps into my body. I can't sleep from the intense pain in my stomach. I've started having symptoms of hepatitis as well, perhaps because of the contaminated water we drank.

I admit it, now I only want to live like other kids, just to have a normal life.

NOUR ASHOUR
20 years old
Jabalia

I used to study law. I have one sister and four brothers. We live in Jabalia – to be precise, in a neighbourhood called Bir al-Naaja, north of the city. I never liked this name, I used to tell people I lived in al-Saftawy. In the past, Jabalia was flooded with lemon and orange groves. My fiancé worked as a doctor in al-Shifa Hospital. We were getting ready to be married and we were furnishing our house, planning it down to the smallest detail.

On 7 October, I was jolted awake, all of Gaza was woken by the booming of the rockets. We tried to go online to learn the specifics. We couldn't believe what was happening. People seemed to have gone mad. Hamas was firing rockets and we didn't know or understand what was going on.

I was 5 years old the first time I saw war. I was in nursery. I had two friends, Farah and Hadeel – we were born in the same week and lived on the same street. Our houses were next door to each other, and we used to wear matching clothes. The nursery was a five-minute walk from home. On our way there, we saw planes for the first time, they were enormous and they bombed like crazy. The noise was terrifying. We were so little and we didn't understand, we just ran home. Our mothers were waiting for us, frightened. That was the 2008 war. The people in our neighbourhood were gathered in one of the neighbours' houses, all making bread together. I remember the mother of one of my friends screaming because her children had been martyred, and meanwhile we kids were screaming and crying, we wanted to eat. The bombing got even crazier, and we screamed even louder, and we were hungry. Since then, I have been very familiar with what bombardment means. In May 2013, our neighbours' house was bombed. I remember that after the son rebuilt it, it wasn't long before bombing destroyed it a second time. Back then, the Israelis would call us to say they were going to bomb, and we would run outside and escape. Previous wars had limits. We've lived through repeated wars in Gaza, short-lived and piecemeal, but this time is different, this isn't war like we're used to. The previous wars were hard, but they would end, and we were able to survive. Food was scarce but it wasn't like this time, we were hungry, but not like this.

After hours of silence and waiting and fear, the bombardment began. Once the resistance fighters were identified, their families were bombed. Then they went into the hospital records, took the names of the wounded and bombed their houses too. Their revenge was barbaric.

I kept sleeping by the window. The sky would light up red and blue from the density of the bombing, I saw missiles falling. People all around were frightened, everyone was falling over themselves to buy tins to store at home. At first it all seemed normal to me – bombardment and destruction are nothing new for us. I would often speak with my fiancé, sometimes we would laugh, and we would pray that our house wouldn't be bombed before we had lived in it. I was a bride preparing for her wedding. We had put all our money into furnishing and renovating our house, from the windows down to the smallest details. Everything was new for us to begin our life together. We never imagined this war would wipe out everything.

Missiles shook the ground like an earthquake, barrel bombs fell on us from the sky. One of them landed on our house. The house wasn't destroyed completely at first, but shrapnel landed everywhere and the windows were shattered. As the bombing intensified, those still alive started to leave in droves, going on foot under bombardment, fleeing at a run. We only stayed in our house for five days after 7 October. Perhaps, because we have grown up under bombardment, I thought that it would all pass like it had done before. Then we were displaced to my uncle's house in Beit Lahia – we believed their area would be safer, as there were still a lot of civilians there. The bombing never stopped, I could always see missiles. During the day I started to take pictures of the children, my sister's children, and then at night I would stay awake so I could take pictures of the bombardment and follow news of the martyrs in our neighbourhood. Death never stopped – what could I do? Everyone around me was dying. How could I deal with such horror?

My friend's husband was martyred, and when she mourned him and put his picture on the internet, I asked her to delete it – I was frightened they would bomb her house. I knew they were watching every single one of us. The children would sleep with their hands over their ears, curled up on themselves, like they were hiding inside their own bodies. The noise of the planes, the smoke, the dust, the screaming – none of it ever stopped. They didn't give us time to catch our breath. They would follow the displaced people and bomb them. Rumours spread, so we went into the open air, afraid. Young and old, we packed our bags and waited in the streets. I wore the same clothes for six months. The electricity was cut off, there was no internet. We would charge our mobile phones at the house of a neighbour who had a small generator.

We no longer knew where we could go. Houses were burning down all around us, and it became a certainty that our turn was coming. Seeing people die like this was a horror I had never experienced before. The explosions still reverberate in my head, even now. My uncle's house in Beit Lahia was next to Kamal Adwan Hospital, and I saw the hospital every day, saw hundreds of corpses with my own eyes. This is not an exaggeration – the corpses there numbered into the hundreds. At first, they would honour the bodies by burying them and bringing them out in ambulances, then they started moving them by donkey cart accompanied by five people, then there was no longer anyone attending any funeral. After that, they stopped removing them at all, and the bodies piled up in the hospital courtyard.

Our neighbour's daughters were martyred. They were from the Abu Saada family, in the al-Fakhoura area of Jabalia. We had left them behind because we were displaced to a different area. Isra, Dalia, Dina, Salam all died, along with their only brother, Fathi Abu Saada, and their mother too. Only Iman and her sister were left alive, it was a massacre. Their father was killed in the 2008 war while he was getting food for his children, and he left behind seven daughters, a son and a pregnant wife. The girls lived without a father, and the mother gave birth to a girl she named Hala, who never knew him. Those girls were hardworking, beautiful and educated. Their mother raised them with her own blood, she was a widow and devoted her whole life to raising them. She bought them a house, and do you know where she chose it? The place where their father was martyred. There, the girls grew up, graduated from university and got married, one after another. That whole family vanished. They couldn't even take their bodies out of the ruins. That massacre took place on 14 October. It was a huge shock to me. I was in my uncle's house by then, and along with seeing the relentless stream of corpses, I began to have a breakdown.

But I told myself I must document everything.

My nephew Udi turned 4. We tried to give the children some happiness to make things easier for them, so we decided to have a birthday party for him under bombardment. Just as we started to blow out the candles, we got news that our house had been bombed. My brothers barely got out before the missile landed. By some miracle they survived, but our neighbours were hit and martyred. No one ate the cake. Udi didn't celebrate his birthday. My sister's friend, Shams al-Lidaway, was martyred with her family in Jabalia. Her father, mother, brothers, sisters and uncle – all of them martyred. Those who were left became amputees.

The bread began to run out, there wasn't even flour to be had any more, and we began to suffer from hunger. At six in the morning, they bombed the house next door. People gathered to rescue the martyrs' bodies, I witnessed it myself, and when the first responders arrived to pull the victims from the rubble, the Israelis saw them and bombed them. Bodies began flying through the air, everywhere, all around. They bombed the ambulance – we saw it happen. Death was everywhere. We thought we were going to die, I was waiting to die, it wasn't just a feeling but a fact. I was totally certain I was going to die. I resigned myself to the will of God and said I would not be preferred over others. We couldn't go anywhere else, we could no longer move. They bombed al-Azhar University. That day, my fiancé sent me a photo from al-Shifa Hospital of a burned girl, she was completely blackened. My fiancé would send me pictures of atrocities so I could document them, and meanwhile I was taking pictures of the atrocities around me. You can't express what happened during that phase, it was impossible to fully document the murders committed by the Israeli army. Fire belts were exploding around us, and after that we lost our hearing. Every day, there were fire belts, and we reached 27 October, and twenty days had passed. I was by the window, photographing a continuous fire belt, and my uncle's wife wet herself from fear and couldn't move. People were running and screaming, limbs were flying. All of this, I could see from the window. That's how the days passed. My father asked me to go out to buy some things. The buildings were destroyed, everything was razed to the ground. The market too – I was stunned by the sight of it, they had bombed it as well. People were calling out to the martyrs, others were carrying their biers and weeping. Death never stopped. My friends from the Afana family were martyred. Saja Afana was my neighbour, we heard of their deaths while we were in my uncle's house. And her brother Muhammad Afana was martyred, he was completely burned and his wife was left behind, only the wife was left alive. My friend Ghadeer's husband died, Ghadeer from the Abu Safiya family, she used to live in Sheikh Radwan and she gave birth the day before her husband was martyred. My friend Lama Abu Eida, who studied engineering, died along with her whole family. So did Wasal al-Nahawy. All of them died, I saw them dead, I saw them with my own eyes. Then my uncle's children were martyred in Nuseirat, we saw them on Al-Jazeera. They never found the body of one of the children, who had been turned into just limbs. Everyone in the house was martyred, including their mother. On my mother's side, my aunt's children were martyred too. I couldn't believe we were still alive when everyone around us was dying. Lana, Lama, Omar and Maryam. Look at these photos, Samar – look at them! They died too! Look at this picture of the plane in the sky, you can see it clearly even though it's night-time. I started to fear the news, because I knew it would bring accounts of more martyrs. A strange feeling of guilt was killing me – everyone around me was dying, while I continued to be alive. I carried on documenting so I could justify my life to myself.

During those days as well, the vegetables ran out and all food disappeared. The price for nine tomatoes was thirty dollars. It was my dream at that stage to eat a zaatar sandwich, imagine! Our life became a heavy burden. My mother spent all day kneading and washing – she never rested. Her hands and fingers were lacerated from so much washing and kneading. When flour was available, we would knead bread and eat it with just salt, because even olive oil and zaatar had disappeared. This was in early November. Then I got stomach pains. There was a well with dirty water, that's where we got our water from. There was no electricity, no clean water, no food. We were drinking this water, and then I started having excruciating stomach pains. I started going to Kamal Adwan Hospital where the rubbish was heaped up in piles, and inside the hospital there were displaced people spread out everywhere, and the place was full of flies. I could see lamb being eaten out of the rubbish, I saw children trying to get hold of some water, even if it was contaminated. I saw a girl carrying an empty water jug and took some photos of her. Everyone was trying to get water by any means possible, but when they drank it, it made them sick.

On 14 November, we began thinking we should leave. The situation had become unbearable. We thought we were going to die of thirst and hunger. Look at this picture, Samar, see how people were fighting and shoving each other over a few drops of water! That was our last day in my uncle's house. The Israelis said they were going to bomb Kamal Adwan Hospital, they were going to enter overland and storm the hospital, and they bombed the surroundings. Staying there was suicide. They bombed schools of displaced people with gas and phosphorus – I took pictures, look! And after they bombed the house next door, we knew we had to leave. The smells in Beit Lahia had become deadly suffocating, and they were causing people to flee. They even made pregnant women pass out. We were forced out to Jabalia Camp, crowds and crowds of us – this was 20 November. We were on our way to my aunt's house when we saw planes bombing the UNRWA clinics in Jabalia. We found my aunt's neighbourhood, which used to be a lively area and had become a complete ruin. And we had barely left Beit Lahia when they bombed my uncle's house – we had once again survived thanks to a miracle. We were fleeing by the skin of our teeth from house to house, we had only been hours ahead of death since the beginning of this war.

I was looking for something that would give me the strength to go on, so I started writing the stories of the people around me. I would observe them and document their lives with words and pictures. The girls gathered round me, and I would join in their conversation. Everyone close to them had lost loved ones, mothers had lost their limbs. I was cautious about telling their stories, because most of the survivors had lost their limbs or their sight. Whole families were annihilated, and sometimes only a single son or daughter was left alive out of a whole family. At that point, we were in my aunt's house in the north, and meanwhile the bombing was getting worse. We took shelter in Yemen Saeed Hospital. It was basically just a clinic, but it became a temporary hospital because of the war. We felt that staying in a hospital might offer us some safety, but we soon realized that there were no safe places, as those very hospitals were targets for the bombing. The hospital was filled with a mixture of displaced people and patients; every corner became a shelter for the injured. We decided to leave, the bombardment was beyond bearing and the whole area was under fire. I was permanently afraid. Every house I left was immediately bombed. We couldn't sleep, we lived in a constant state of wakefulness, especially as my aunt was sick with diabetes and we had other extremely ill patients with us too. We stayed in Jabalia Camp, where my aunt couldn't move because of her health. It hurt to see her screaming, unable to move, and we couldn't do a thing.

After we left Jabalia we went to an area called al-Dabbabat. We were forced to go via Salah al-Din Road – this is one of the principal roads in Gaza, next to al-Bahr Street. Salah al-Din Road was known for connecting different parts of Gaza. In front of us was an Israeli checkpoint known as Khatt al-Mawt.* It was close to where I studied, al-Azhar University. The area had turned into a battlefield: Israeli forces were concentrated there, having raised a huge Israeli flag, set up checkpoints and built sand ramparts. The soldiers were wearing sand-coloured uniforms, which made them hard to see. The area was full of guns and tanks, and there was a 'detention yard' where they gathered people. When we passed through these forces in convoys, I felt enormously insulted. We were literally forced into humiliation, they were yelling at us and ordering us to raise our hands and feet like we were slaves. I heard curses and insults from the soldiers: *Get moving you animals, move it you donkeys, on your knees, hands up.* I hadn't agreed with the decision to go south, I felt crushed and preferred death over being exposed to such humiliation. But my uncle's wife was ill, and people all around me were crying and shouting. Even though I was against

* Khatt al-mawt translates as 'the line of death'.

displacement, the family took a joint decision, because the situation was unbearable. My father also refused to move, he said, 'If a tank is at the door I will die in my home, honourably.' I tried to convince him not to leave, but for the first time he found himself overwhelmed and powerless. He had to make a fateful decision that would determine the lives of fourteen people, the entire family. In the end, we were all stood wondering: where will we go? Especially as everywhere was already full with displaced people.

We decided to take my brother's wife to her family home, and my uncle's wife and her children to their uncles' house, and then it was just the five of us: me, my parents and my brothers. We abandoned our large houses, and now we were walking towards the unknown. I hated my feelings. We left without taking anything with us. I left my bridal jihaz* and all my things, we left everything, we only took the clothes we were wearing. The Israeli soldiers were stopping children from crying and threatening women, saying: *Shut your kids up or we'll shoot them*. We saw all this humiliation while we were passing them, how can I forget? We really were hungry, and I was so sad I no longer knew how to cry.

It was all madness. I can't convey the loss. I always say, 'I don't want people to die, I want them to stay alive.' I reject the idea of sacrificing people's lives for anything, I don't want them to die. Some of the people were trying to maintain a little composure. We spent three hours at the checkpoint, and I had my brother's children with me. I was so frightened for my brother's son because he didn't show any reaction. I tried to explain to him what was happening, and I told him that we would be facing the Israeli

* Jihaz – trousseau: the clothes, linen and general household possessions that a bride prepares for her married life.

soldiers. The soldiers separated us, they were searching us and splitting up families. Some families lost each other at the checkpoint, and no one was allowed to object. We lost some of the children and we were terrified of being separated as had happened in old stories of the Nakba,* when people lost each other. The Israelis didn't care. When I was at the checkpoint, I opened my phone and looked at a photo of my fiancé, I was frightened by all the madness that was happening, and terrified I would hear news of his death. I started crying, and the Israelis kept tormenting us while we were crossing. My family stayed on the other side of the checkpoint. We were so scared of losing each other. After two hours under the burning sun, my mother arrived at last and we were back together. We were genuinely overjoyed to be meeting again. We had to keep going south, but there were no cars or buses, people were travelling by donkey cart. It was like living in a past century. We were heading south in convoy towards Rafah, people on donkey carts. As for me, I didn't ride in one – in fact, I stood there, looking around at what was happening, I couldn't believe it. Eventually a small, ancient bus came and its driver demanded a huge amount to take us, even though he was from Gaza. We were forced to pay five hundred dollars.

In Rafah, we had to divide the family across several houses. The situation was ridiculous and painful at the same time: families on top of families in cramped houses. I noticed my grandmother had shrunk, and my brother's wife had changed colour. Their faces were thin and withered, as if in a short space of time we had become vagrants. Our faces grew haggard and pale, our

---

* The events surrounding the 1948 Arab-Israeli War are referred to by Palestinians as 'the Nakba', or 'the catastrophe', as a result of the vast scale of violence and displacement that was perpetrated.

bodies skinny and unfamiliar. My brothers had heard that the house we'd stayed in had been bombed, and so they thought we had died. Yes, we had been in that house, but we had left it before it was bombed. Like I said, this isn't just a story, it's the truth. It seems like stories out of a book, but it's what happened to us. We survived thanks to a miracle, and at that moment, a strange moment, we all felt happy. Me, my mother and father, my brothers, the whole family, we felt deeply content. We had survived! I remember ridiculous moments in the middle of our displacement journey, when we arrived at my aunt's house. I was starving and I could smell delicious food, I thought I was about to faint from hunger. It was the smell of bread and oil, zaatar and tomatoes and cucumber. I seemed to be smelling it for the first time in my life. We suddenly turned into aliens – had we ever really eaten this food? I spent a long time sniffing the cucumber and tomatoes, as if I had never encountered such a fragrance before. I lost all memory of smell and flavour, I forgot how food tasted. I was savouring bread as if I had never tasted it before, and I kept smelling my fingers after every bite. My joy was indescribable.

I remember another occasion, when my brother's son Udi came up to me with a pale face, and said very seriously, 'Auntie, is God stronger than Spiderman?' I replied, 'Yes, God is stronger than anything.' Then he asked, 'Why does He let them kill us if He is stronger than them?' I laughed, but in the moment I didn't know how to reply. When we got to my aunt's house in the south, the bombing was still going on but it was a bit lighter. We found a small warehouse that my aunt owned, so we started to clean it and arrange it into a temporary place for us. There were still some vegetables in the markets but they were very expensive. At that time – it was November

– the crowding hadn't become so intense yet. The situation soon changed and things became catastrophically worse, but despite everything we managed to hang on.

I started to write about what was happening around me. I never thought I would write, I was a law student and never had anything to do with writing. At first I would observe people. Each one of them had a horrific story. I wrote one story and published it on my Twitter account, and it got a lot of engagement. After that, I realized I could convey people's suffering, and that's how I started to notice the stories no one had talked about before, for various reasons. I wrote about the lack of sanitary towels for women, something that perhaps no one thinks about in the middle of war, but it's a real ordeal. I also wrote about the lack of nappies for babies, and about other details that usually aren't touched on in times like these. I suddenly realized that these details are very important – they affect people's lives. We were sleeping on tiles, drinking polluted water, eating unsanitary food and living in the middle of bombardment. I spoke about girls and how the bathrooms in areas of displacement aren't fit for use, a bathroom of one metre square used by thousands of people! There are girls taking pills to postpone their periods so they can avoid embarrassment and suffering – yes, that happened. I wrote about this so I could turn people's attention to vital needs that are often ignored. I have no connection to politics, I was just telling the stories of the people around me. Each person had a story that deserved to be told. My story was the most ordinary. Only the stories I wrote made me feel as though I was keeping people alive, somehow. Yes, the world must not forget them. I try to write people's stories, and I want people to hear my story, because I am one of them. The only difference is I am still alive.

208

AHMED ABU RADWAN
30 years old
Jabalia Camp

I used to work in a restaurant, then in a supermarket. I changed jobs a lot, actually. I work so I can eat. I didn't study and I didn't finish my education. Social Affairs in Gaza offered me a small kiosk business in Jabalia Camp, then I expanded.

I don't know how to talk about what happened, but I'll try.

I was injured on 8 October, the second day of the war, at ten in the morning. My family and I just finished breakfast. I went out of the house and immediately saw bombing. The ground shook like a powerful earthquake, as if it was going to split apart. I froze at first and said, 'This is Judgement Day.'

They fired many huge missiles at us, and then next thing I knew I was running alongside people. Everyone around me was running, we couldn't see in front of us. I was running and shouting, calling for my brothers and sisters, looking for them. There were twelve of us: eight boys and four girls. My father was a regular employee at Jawwal.* My mother was a housewife who never went outside, and she was very sick – she suffered from pulmonary fibrosis and had lived on oxygen since before the war. My brothers and their wives and children, none of them are left. They were all martyred. What can I say about them? They were all martyred with their children. They all passed away in the bombing. It all happened so suddenly.

I can't speak...

I didn't hear the bomb. The missiles landed after I left

* A communications company based in Palestine.

the house. I didn't understand that they had struck our house, because at that point I was in the street. I didn't die, by some miracle I survived. Just a few minutes earlier I had been sitting with them, then I went out to the street. Later on, it became clear that there were some missiles next to our house and other missiles that actually hit our house, and I couldn't understand it. How can you? Eighteen members of my family died all at once. My father buried his brothers, his sons and their wives, and his grandchildren. When he left the cemetery after burying his grandchildren and his children and his brother's wives, he had a stroke. Now he is disabled and paralysed at the European Hospital in Rafah.

I survived, but I lost my leg. My leg was amputated three times. There were maggots coming out of it. I still remember how the ground shook. I imagined that the strike hit our neighbours, but it was our house, where we used to sit on the ground floor with my siblings and their children and their wives, as we did every day. Suddenly they were gone.

Diab, Wasim, Mahmoud, Muhammad, Fady, Wissam, Riham and Nabila. All of them from the Abu Radwan family, all of them dead.

During the bombing, I got myself out from under the rubble and saw my leg was cut off, it was gone from below the knee. They took me to the Indonesian Hospital. I wasn't alone, and even though my leg was severed they didn't consider my case to be critical. There were people there who were torn to shreds, so they decided to come back to me. They gave me some first aid and disinfected the wound, then they left me and were busy with the people who were torn to pieces.

The Israelis entered the Indonesian Hospital in the middle of November. I was on an upper floor, and there

210

was a massacre. First they bombed us, then they entered. We were living alongside displaced people and they admitted me to intensive care. We were afraid of the Israelis, and people were fleeing the hospital. Intensive care was filled with amputees. I was best off, just one leg missing. Israeli soldiers came in and took the doctors. They screamed, beat people and arrested the wounded, and at one in the morning they withdrew.

In the morning, we left the hospital and we saw the fourteen people they had arrested – their bodies had been left in front of the hospital gate. It was an awful sight. I decided to leave the hospital, as I was convinced they were coming back to kill us as well.

The bombing never stopped, and we no longer gave it much thought. We lived under the shadow of death all the time. From 8 October to the middle of November, while I was in hospital, I stopped feeling pain. When they told me that maggots were crawling out of my body, I just looked without caring.

The Red Crescent transferred me to the European Hospital in Khan Younis. On the way there, an Israeli checkpoint stopped us and set dogs on us, even though we were all in a critical condition. They kept us at the checkpoint for hours, and I could see the bodies of women and children on both sides of the road. Even though the Red Crescent had coordinated our transportation and we were travelling in their ambulances, the Israelis still stopped us, searched us and tortured us.

When we reached the European Hospital, they told me they were going to amputate my leg a second time, and that I might die. Every time a piece of my leg was amputated, the infection spread further and further, and there was no solution apart from amputating the whole thing. And because I have diabetes, that made things even more difficult. I stayed in the European Hospital for thirty days. They amputated my leg three times until there was nothing left of it. The first amputation was below the knee, now it's below the pelvis. I have seen myself dying while I am alive, I've learned how the human body decomposes when we die.

The Israeli army doesn't bomb house by house, they bomb whole areas, as if they've decided to completely erase a group of buildings from existence. All the while, people's bodies were disappearing and their body parts were getting mixed with iron and cement, and there was no way of finding their remains after that. Death is everywhere. We were used to minor wars, to small doses of death, but not like this.

I've lived through three wars before. At first we thought this war would be like the others, they would strike military locations or target Hamas. But this time they've left nothing. I don't believe they will stop.

Yes, I've lost my leg, I've lost my family, I've lost everything, there's nothing more that can be said. I don't know why I'm telling you all this. I shouldn't be saying anything.

How can you speak about all this?

You can't.

S
34 years old

Are you asking about what happened on 7 October? I think you have enough responses about what you want to hear. But I only remember a single point of light. I spent twenty hours buried under rubble. You know the story, Samar; there's a bombing, the Israelis fire a missile onto a building full of people, the building collapses and is erased from existence and the rubble gets mixed with people's bodies. Like others, I was one of the people buried under a collapsing building. My husband and three of my children died. They never found them, they searched for a long time but it was no use. It was only after a week I learned they never found them.

Do you believe in miracles, Samar? I do. Alhamdulillah, I am content with the fate God has written for me. If it wasn't for my faith in God, and my fear of His punishment, perhaps I would kill myself. Sometimes I think it would be better if I had died with my husband and children. There's no way of changing anything in the world. I don't ask for anything. I don't remember many details. Even my children's faces are vanishing from my memory. I look at pictures of them so I don't lose my memory of what they looked like.

I used to have three daughters, all of them were beautiful and hard-working at school. The oldest was 15, a very diligent girl, I raised her to be strong and she knew how to say no. After her came my 13-year-old daughter, then the youngest who was 10. I only remember simple things. We were like many families in Gaza, we lived in one building with the whole family – family was very important to us. We would unite as a family, and the relatives would help each other in their misfortunes. So we all came together:

213

me, my brothers, my mother, the grandchildren and my father. An ideal, close-knit family. My mother and father survived, but my three brothers and their wives and children all died.

Of 7 October itself, I remember most that illuminated spot: a circular light amid the darkness I was trapped in for twenty hours. I was buried in the wreckage. I couldn't move so much as a hand. Only my head was in a small space, and thanks to that, it was written that I should live. That space contained a narrow passage like a cord of light, and that's how air and light came and filled the circle containing my head.

I am the oldest sister in the family. They married me off when I was 17. I didn't say no. Anything they thought would benefit the family, I would do. They decided I should leave school and get married. We were four girls and three boys. The girls came first, and we were raised to be mothers to our brothers. I had no objection, I would do anything to please my mother. That was the way of things in our family, and in our society. I never, ever refused a demand. Marriage was sutra* for a girl. And I was supposed to have children, so I did. I devoted all my energies to pleasing my mother. That's how we were raised: to serve our male brothers. And I did it with love. Sutra, a good reputation, pleasing God and pleasing my parents – these were the priorities.

I decided to finish my education after I was married. I was very young, but I loved writing. I wanted to be a writer. I loved reading, and after the obligations of the house and the children, I spent all my spare time reading, everything my eye fell on. So I studied at university after

---

* Sutra: literally, a cover or a screen. In this context, S is referring to marriage as a form of protection for a girl, both to provide her with a shelter and to preserve her chastity.

I finally managed to get my husband and family to agree. I spent years trying to convince them, and when they agreed – with many conditions – I finished my education. I completed a specialization of Arabic Language at university and I wanted to study journalism. But my mother saw what I was doing as a source of shame and lack of faith. She said my husband was a good man because he allowed me to study, and that was enough. They wouldn't let me work.

I had given birth to three girls, and they asked me to have another, because I should have a boy. In their eyes, my motherhood wasn't complete unless I had a boy. My husband said he wanted a boy. I said to them, 'As you wish.' So I was pregnant when they bombed us. I was in my fourth month on the day of the explosion.

You want to know what happened on 7 October? I'll tell you, even though I am still trying to understand it all. I was furious at everything around me: at the burdens of the house, the children, the never-ending wars, the siege, even at my mother and my husband. I wanted to study journalism, but they stopped me. I was writing – I have a notebook I am always filling with words and ideas. I would buy notebooks from the bookshop, I would read books on the internet, I would follow what was happening in the world. I never told anyone what I wrote, we weren't allowed to speak about what we saw: about pain, rape, harassment. I would read and write, but I didn't dare breathe a word.

Perhaps I was a coward, but I will change – or perhaps I've changed already, after that illuminated spot that saved my life, and the moment I heard my mother's voice as she was walking next to me while I was buried under the rubble.

I already told you I spent twenty hours in the rubble, and I couldn't speak. I was screaming inside, trying to move my lips, but my voice wouldn't come out and I couldn't even move my body. I just heard them, moving around nearby. Suddenly I heard my mother's voice – here she was, really close. My heart set on fire. I wanted to scream, 'I'm here!' But she was only calling the names of my brothers. I said to myself, 'She'll remember me soon, she'll call my name.' But the footsteps came and went, came and went, and my mother kept looking for her male children.

Was she only looking for them? She was walking with the first responders, then she left. I am trying to remember – did she come a second time? Or was it just a dream? Did I really hear her voice? Did she ever call for me or my sisters? I don't think she did. Even now, I can't believe it. She was calling the names of my three brothers, over and over, and I heard sobbing. If she had called my name, even once, life would have been different. But that didn't happen. She carried on repeating my brothers' names until she disappeared.

They saved me later on. How? By pure chance! The debris around me collapsed, and they found me. I was unconscious. When I opened my eyes, I saw shadows before I closed them again. I didn't ask about my daughters or my husband. I didn't say a word for over a month. My leg was amputated, and four fingers, there was no time to think of anything. We were moving from one hospital to another, from displacement to displacement. I don't want to repeat what you already know about the genocide we faced. The Israelis never stopped bombing, they would re-bomb corpses and break them apart.

I still wonder how my mother could do that. I've never asked her, and I never will. My three brothers died, they were like sons to me. This memory is all I have left of 7 October: the spot of light that enveloped my head, and my mother's voice as she called only for my brothers. I am still alive, with roughly half a body. One day I will write about everything, but not now. I will wait until my mother departs this life. Until that time, don't mention who I am or where I'm from. I don't even want to say the names of my beautiful girls. I want to forget.

Did you know I was four months pregnant? Did I tell you that? They had wanted a boy to carry on his father's name. What about the baby? It died. It died straight away. I miscarried, he died in my belly. That's another story.

BUSHRA AL-GHALBAN ABU SABIH
42 years old
Khan Younis

We live in Ma'an, one of the villages to the east of Khan Younis. I studied English Language at university, and in 2004 I got a job at UNRWA, and I still work there now. I have spent twenty years working in various schools.

This war hasn't left anything of Khan Younis, they have completely destroyed the city. I don't know how to describe 7 October. It was a normal day. My husband, an orthopaedic doctor at Nasser Hospital, was getting ready to go to work, and we were getting ready to go to school. We finished getting ready and dressed and we were just about to leave when we heard a boom, and then saw the rockets being fired. By virtue of our experience with previous wars, we knew there wouldn't be school that day, but things didn't stop there. There weren't just intermittent missiles as there had been previously – total war broke out.

We were worried because we realized that this war would be completely different from everything we'd been through. We stayed in our houses, and even though we knew the war would be worse than anything we'd experienced before, we never expected what happened afterwards. Everything we witnessed would surpass comprehension. Do we call it genocide? Even this word doesn't seem sufficient to describe what took place. There are many things I want to talk about, but words fail me. Sometimes I think it's not an appropriate time to speak about hope or grief or even our personal feelings. Perhaps it is better to simply relate what happened to all of us, or perhaps I should even be silent. But I want to share what I saw. Please, write down every word.

On the first day, 7 October, they bombed the tower blocks in Gaza, and by the end of the day the bombing reached Khan Younis. The bombing became routine, and we began to expect the arrival of missiles at any moment. They targeted buildings without sending warnings to the civilians, as they had done in previous wars. My husband is a doctor and I am a teacher, we are normal people, like most people living in Gaza. On 24 October, we heard the sound of a nearby strike and we saw smoke and dust and the marks of destruction. Even so, we went back to sleep, as the war had become a normal part of life by then. I am mother to three sons and a daughter, and my children are always with me, I am never apart from them. My oldest son was studying at university and he sent us pictures of a bombed-out house, the house of Um Mahmoud Shirab. Do you know why they bombed her house? In the 2014 war, her son who was with the resistance was killed, and ever since they have targeted the homes of the martyrs' families, people who lost their children in previous wars. Their revenge is blind, they even target the dead and aspire to wipe out their families. The missile that fell on Um Mahmoud's house didn't explode, but it made a big hole, and after that people fled the area. We were learning that revenge would have no limits.

We were no longer capable of expecting anything but the worst, especially after our neighbours' house adjoining ours was bombed at random. I thought I was safe, we had made our house a refuge for displaced people. I believed they would never bomb our house because we have no connection to the resistance or to Hamas, but we were forced to leave it and go to my family's house. After we left, they bombed our neighbour's house at night and levelled it, and our house was also damaged. They struck us with barrel bombs, not ordinary missiles. At that time,

219

we were still only experiencing the aerial assault, the ground assault hadn't reached Khan Younis.

We were forced out of our home on 6 December. The bombs were falling all around us, and I thought I was going to die with my family. Displacement was just another delusion – there was no safe place to go, because everywhere was being bombed. We remained somewhere in between life and death until the ground war began. We observed everything that was happening around us, we saw the atrocities they committed on the ground. They divided the Strip into blocks and put a map on it and gave every area a number. They claimed, falsely, that they would uphold humanitarian law. The area of Khan Younis, which includes al-Qarara – or as we say, Karara with a K – was one of those areas. Our turn came, block 45 in the Ma'an district. It's an eastern village, a huge agricultural area with a few scattered houses – there is no resistance there.

They dropped leaflets, in very poor Arabic, saying: *To the residents of Ma'an and Karara: you are in a zone of intense fighting, stay safe and leave the area*, and: *You have been warned.*

After reading them, we decided to leave our basically-destroyed house. We took our basic necessities and fled to my family's house.

That night, there was what they call a fire belt. Extremely violent, non-stop bombing on a single area, dozens of missiles and sonic bombs that make a terrifying noise, like the sound of hell. The sparks and the fires turned night into day, the bombs provoked horror everywhere. Khan Younis Camp was built during the Nakba, in 1948. My family used to live in this camp, and next to it is Nasser Hospital, where my husband works. I stayed with my children in my family's house. We moved by donkey cart because it was no longer possible to use cars. My sister and I were displaced to our family when the fire belt began. People barely had time to read the leaflets before the bombardment started, so they fled to a nearby school. In the morning, at around six o'clock, tank bombs were fired at a nearby cultural centre, and an UNRWA school was also targeted. There was no one in the school but civilians. They knew that, just as they knew the school belonged to UNRWA. The drone was hovering constantly, watching people's movements, speaking to them and killing them, and meanwhile the displaced people didn't understand what was happening because of the non-stop bombing and random murders.

It was very strange: drones would kill people and then give them instructions! Everyone was in a state of horror – they had thought they would be safe in an UNRWA school. On 6 December, the Israelis bombed Ma'an Co-educational Preparatory School, an UNRWA school, killing 30 or 35 people. Among the victims were ten members of the al-Ghalban family, my own family: my mother-in-law, my brothers-in-law, my daughter's fiancé, my sister's husband. They were all civilians, sheltering in the school after their houses were bombed, people who had already survived death several times.

This time the bombs didn't come from planes, but from tank cannons which took direct aim at the school. It was no mistake. That bombing was intentional – they saw everything for themselves. Not content with that, they dispatched quadcopters afterwards, drones that target people fleeing. No one was allowed to survive, and that is how all my family members were killed. Murder came from every direction. Dr Ibrahim al-Ghalban, one of the al-Ghalban family – a drone targeted him and killed him. His wife, Ghanima, was standing at the door to their house, and when she saw her husband bleeding, she tried to save him but the drone killed her too. She died at once, next to him, while he kept bleeding until his life ran out. The bodies of Dr Ibrahim and his wife stayed in the square for two whole weeks. No one dared go near them to bury them, because the drones kept killing anyone who got close. The bombing continued without pause, and the drones prevented any movement. Everyone remained a prisoner inside what remained of their destroyed homes.

Dr Ibrahim al-Ghalban was in his sixties, very respected, well-known in his neighbourhood for his work and his morals. The manner of his death, out in front of everyone, was horrendous. People could see him slowly decomposing and couldn't do anything about it. Saddest of all was his brother, who kept looking from his balcony towards Dr Ibrahim's corpse, unable to move or to do anything. Dr Ibrahim's second brother couldn't bear it: he had a stroke from profound grief at what had happened to his brother. Dr Ibrahim's daughter also saw how his body was left in the square, in view of everyone. This situation continued for a fortnight until a member of the Red Cross intervened, and they were able to move the bodies of the civilians. They had stayed in the open air all that time without a funeral or any mark of respect, long after their bodies had decomposed.

On 26 December, they dropped leaflets over my family's house, demanding that we displace once again. They never stopped. The quadcopters came back to spread terror, flying and moving and bombing. We lived under siege even down to the air we breathed, because those mechanical murderers surrounded us. We were trapped, we couldn't move. Even if we wanted to leave to get water, we were frightened a drone would kill us. We were thirsty. We stayed like that, crowded into my family home which

222

was full of displaced people, including us. We were like prisoners, and we accepted we could die at any moment.

My aunt had an intense terror of the quadcopters. We would try and calm her and get her to understand that we had closed all the doors and windows. But she kept saying this flying killer could take voice prints, and could follow everything and execute us. We would turn off our phones for fear of being tracked. We heard stories about zannanat entering houses, one woman saw a drone trying to get in her house through the balcony as she hung up washing. The zannanat targeted people, singling them out and killing them. They killed a five-year-old girl. We had no idea why these drones killed a child of that age. All of this, we saw with our own eyes.

We tried to leave at dawn to buy some things for the house. But as time went on, there were no more markets, or things to buy. The shelves were empty, the food ran out, there was no food available. We paid double to get the barest minimum. We had no food, water or electricity in Khan Younis. On 26 December, after they dropped the leaflets, I left my family home and we went south to Rafah. All this time, we had known that wherever we displaced to, its turn would also come, but we had no other choice. We fled, and we didn't know where we were going. We arrived in Rafah, I had my sister and her husband and her seven children with me, we were a large group. Families began to congregate, we couldn't leave anyone on their own. My brother-in-law's daughter, Amina, had come to Khan Younis on foot from Ma'an and she stayed with us. We welcomed her there, my family welcomed us all. When we decided to go to Rafah, they came with us. We found a house that consisted of a single room, and all of us piled into it. We lived squeezed in together and we didn't know what was happening in Ma'an because it was a blackout area. Later, we heard the Israelis had withdrawn and that all our houses had been destroyed.

My son was suffering from a problem in his ear. It got worse after the bombing because of the intensity of the noise and the widespread bacteria. Hepatitis spread – there are 800,000 displaced people, people are piled on top of each other, infection spreads quickly. The most dangerous thing is hepatitis, and my son was particularly affected in his previously injured ear. In the end, *we lived* – me and my children – we are alive.

BARA HAMADA
17 years old
Sheikh Radwan

On the morning of 7 October, I was getting ready to go to school as usual. All of a sudden, just as I was about to leave the house, we heard the explosions from the rockets Hamas had fired. My mother, Iman, was a teacher. She was preparing my little brothers for school and getting ready to go to work. We would usually leave together every morning. My mother used to work at Huda High School for Girls, and as for my father, he was an administrative employee at another school. But that morning wasn't like any other day. When we heard the boom, we stayed put and didn't go to school. Intense bombing started up in the afternoon, and it never stopped after that. We all stayed at home. Days went by and we were living in the middle of bomb blasts. Sometimes we went out, my dad and I, to buy things we needed for the house, until the day our neighbour's house was bombed and their son was martyred. We realized then that our area – Ard al-Shanti in Sheikh Radwan – was being targeted, all of it, and we had to leave straight away. We left for my grandfather's house in Burj al-Shifa, where we all gathered, the whole family, including my father's sisters and their children. There were about forty-five of us in a five-storey building with two apartments on each floor, all crammed into limited space.

On the night of 5 November, at one in the morning, the men were sleeping in one area, the children in one room and the women in another. We were piled into the place, and the sound of the bombing never stopped, and meanwhile the tanks were getting closer. Suddenly, glass went flying and everywhere filled up with dust, then the walls collapsed. Four missiles fell onto the building in succession, I felt the earth shake beneath us like it was swaying. When the bomb hit me, I felt intense pain, and I heard my mother's voice saying to me, 'Recite the shahada! Recite the shahada!' She thought I was dying. My feet were torn to pieces. At the time I didn't realize my foot had been severed, I only learned that later on, when I understood that the missile had hit my leg. While I was still in a state of shock, people picked me up and carried me out only to find the stairs blocked with debris. Glass was embedded too deeply in my back to be taken out, and fifteen people from the journalist Muhammad Jaja's family were martyred in that building. Only a 2-year-old girl survived. When my mother took me to the first responders, she gave them my foot. They took it and buried it with the remains and body parts of the other victims, I never found out where. In the hospital, they performed surgery on me while my mother waited for me in the Reception Department, sitting on the floor surrounded by blood and body parts. She witnessed victims arriving from another massacre, in al-Shati Camp.

When I woke up later on, I learned that I had lost my leg. I was 16 years old. I blacked out from shock for a few minutes. After the surgery, my mother entered a state of dread and started to search among the bodies for my little brother, thinking he had been lost. It was an unforgettable scene – she told me afterwards that for a moment, she thought she had lost her mind.

I stayed in al-Shifa Hospital for seventeen days. I struggled with pain and fear amid non-stop bombing, even bombing on the hospital itself. One day, Friday 10 November, bombs hit the maternity ward, and I wasn't expecting to leave the hospital alive. But I stayed till the end. The Burno Mosque opposite the hospital was bombed, and bombs started to rain down on us, so my family quickly picked me up and put me in a different room. That was on a Friday, and the bombing was everywhere, above and around us. I thought my heart was going to stop from the intensity of the pain, and I was screaming constantly, I couldn't control it. They changed my dressings without anaesthetic – they used a medicine called ketamine but it had absolutely no effect on me. I asked them to amputate my other leg because I couldn't stand the pain. In the middle of all this, the Israeli soldiers fired tear gas at us, and there were quadcopters firing towards our rooms, so we left as quickly as we could. The gas was suffocating, bullets pierced the walls. We didn't know where we were heading. Everyone began running like it was the moment of Hashr. The doctors actually left, the trainees made do with just trying to care for the wounded. They had nothing but vinegar with which to sterilize, so maggots started appearing in my wounds, and no one could do anything. The whole hospital was completely under siege, Israeli tanks and guns surrounded the place.

This situation continued for two weeks until they decided to storm the hospital. We were living on very little food and drink, and I saw lots of deaths around me. My mother was terrified my wounds would become septic and kill me. She would check on me and say, 'I will never leave you, I will stay with you.' Orders came to evacuate the hospital and they demanded everyone who remained behind assemble on the first floor. They took me down in my bed because no one was allowed to stay on the upper floors. We all assembled on the first floor. The quadcopters were hovering over us and shooting, soldiers stormed the hospital. They began rounding up all the healthy young men, they took them away and made them get undressed and blindfolded them, and all the while I was waiting in my bed. They interrogated my mother and asked her why I was injured, and she stood up to them fiercely, saying, 'You're the ones who did this to him!' It was a week of continual horror. Afterwards, they opened the lifts and brought guns into the hospital. Then we saw some of the men swapping their civilian clothes for military clothes and taking photos as though they were part of Hamas. We didn't know the purpose of these pictures. They brought us food and took photos of us as though they were offering us help, and the following day they forced us to leave the food and throw it away, even though we were starving.

We never saw any person from Hamas, but the soldiers asked about them continually. I tried to understand the reason for all this focus, without coming up with an explanation. The Israeli soldiers asked me about my injury and my life and my family, many details, and in the end I told them, 'This is all I know, I'm only sixteen.' We left the hospital after that and spent a whole day on the road. We spent hours at the checkpoint on our way to the European Hospital. A new problem faced me at the checkpoint, because the Israeli soldiers thought I was one of their hostages. Apparently I look like one of them. I kept confirming to them, over and over, that I was Palestinian, but they took no notice. Perhaps their doubt was due to my appearance – because I'm fair, with light hair and blue eyes, they didn't easily believe it. They began interrogating me, and after they were convinced I really was Palestinian and not one of the hostages they were looking for, they started to beat me and insult me. They put guns against my amputated leg and beat me. After that, we reached Nasser Hospital in Khan Younis. We had to spend the whole night lying on tiles in the cold until the following morning, when they admitted us into a large hall divided up with curtains. That was the hospital they put us in. I was still in a serious state. My amputated leg wouldn't stop bleeding, I almost died because I didn't receive the necessary treatment, and all I could think of was how would I be able to walk later on? How would I go back to school, how would I go to university with one leg that can hardly move? The thought of the future terrifies me. I wonder how I will stand up, what I will do. Things in the south weren't much better than the north. True, we've escaped the massacres there, but the suffering continues. The hardest moment by far was when I learned I had lost my leg. I still remember it. I cried so much, because my dream was to study dentistry, and along with learning I'd lost many of my friends, including Abdel Rahman and Malik, I felt a huge void. I love swimming, I used to swim twice a week. I wonder now, can I swim with one leg? My other leg is also damaged, so I don't even know whether it's possible any more.

FIRAS SHEIKH RADWAN
21 years old
Gaza City

Before I became a half-person, as I am now, I was studying Accounting at the Open University of Jerusalem. I lived in Gaza with my family: a mother, two brothers, a sister and a father who was permanently abroad for his work in commerce. A small family, as you can see, but it was a happy family, or at least that's how I remember it. I was born in war and siege, true, but I loved my university and my studies.

I went to sleep on Friday 6 October, imagining that the following day would be just a normal Saturday, a new academic day. I was woken by the sound of rockets, abruptly cutting off sleep. Intense, excessive noise made me leap out of bed and run downstairs into the street. People all around were in a state of agitation. None of us knew what was happening. At first we thought *we* were being bombed. This is the logic of things in the Strip, that we are bombed. We have grown used to it, just as we have grown used to siege and to patience. But it was different this time – the rockets were coming from us. The neighbours said, 'Soon the Israelis will start one of their usual bombing rounds, a strike or two or three.' Others said, 'No, this is the battle for the liberation of Palestine.' Others declared, 'It won't be an ordinary war,' and others agreed, 'This time, they will kill us all.' Everyone was saying something, and each one of them had a different opinion. Certainly, at least at first, we didn't know what was happening, and we never imagined what was going to occur. I don't remember exactly how the first hours and days passed. What I do remember is that we decided to stay at home. We didn't leave, the Israeli bombing was inevitably on its way, this was a natural part of our lives, this is the logic of things in Gaza. There would be a typical bout of bombardment, one strike, two, three strikes, but in its minutest details, life would go on as normal.

Three days later, on 10 October, we were at home – my mother in one room, me in my room, my siblings in another room, my father abroad – when the Israeli attack began. We had been under siege for two years, we are lacking everything. We are in a chronic war that consumes us slowly. The bombing came and it seemed to me that the only difference was that this time, it was at maximum intensity, and it was never interrupted. It left none of us a chance to even think of leaving. Our neighbour's building was bombed with a heavy calibre missile. Their building was directly behind ours and naturally our house received an abundance of shrapnel and debris from the blast. That was my first injury, in the back. In the moment of being hit I didn't feel any pain, actually I couldn't feel anything at all. When I looked at a photo of my split-open back and examined the flesh and bone, it felt like looking at someone else, like a surgeon performing an operation. A strange feeling, I still don't understand it, so I don't think I'm qualified to describe it. I stared at my neighbours' faces as they carried me to hospital. At that moment, I began to review our decision to stay. The residents of our building were doctors and engineers, my father worked in trade as I told you, all of us were civilians, and there were no fighters from Hamas or any of the other resistance factions among us. The neighbours helped me to al-Shifa Hospital. It was crowded with the injured. Despite its name,* it was lacking many medical necessities and equipment. Once there, I began

* Al-Shifa means convalescence or healing.

to feel pain, my wound was long and deep. I consented for them to close it with old surgical stitches. I didn't have a choice, I wanted to be done as quickly as possible so I could go back to check on everyone. The doctors said I had to stay, but I was preoccupied with thoughts of my family, and I wasn't going to sleep on the ground in the middle of piles of injured people. I left, I don't know how I did it, I don't remember. I do remember that I was staggering and could hardly see. I passed by a pharmacy to buy some iodine disinfectant and gauze, and when I finally got home I found my family were all fine, and the Israelis had issued a statement after the bombing, demanding that we go south to Rafah.

We left, me and my mother and my siblings, we were displaced to a family friend's house on Jala Street in the centre of Gaza City. There, on 25 October , we were caught by new bombardment, and I was injured a second time. Please understand that when I say 'new bombardment', it does not merely signify a numerical repetition. No! This was something different, they call it a fire belt, it's not one or two missiles – it's dozens of rockets and bombs. When this happens, violent, continuous bombardment lasts perhaps a full hour, but this hour lasts forever. Savage bombardment, not content with anything less than wiping away entire neighbourhoods, erasing whole families from the civil register. I was in the street when it began. You can't believe it, you can't describe it. I was in the street when there was a boom and the ground shook and the buildings collapsed. I went upstairs straight away to check on the family and bring them outside. Something indescribable. A mythical bombardment that never paused, buildings crumbling like castles made of biscuit. Everything was shaking: buildings, the ground, our hearts, the air, the people. We were running,

I was running, people all around were running, and while we were running, we saw wreckage, dead people, human body parts scattered everywhere. We no longer saw bodies or heaped clusters, but organs, guts, limbs. I saw some living people too – yes, I saw people who were injured but still had a spark of life. I still remember their faces, children, women, flung here and there. I saw heads, hands, legs; I saw half-bodies, quarter-bodies; I saw bodies opened up like an atlas of anatomy. We were jumping over them, sometimes we trampled on them, sometimes we tripped over them. We trampled on each other, we scrambled and jostled without thinking of anything but escaping the hell whose name is 'fire belt'. It's hideous. Two hundred people were killed all at once, and afterwards that number increased to three hundred. They named that day Khabta al-Jala – the massacre of Jala. My family survived the first wave of fire belts, and we intended to head to the south of the Strip.

My mother, brother and sister got into one car, and I got into the car behind with my second brother. On the way to Rafah, our convoy was bombed. I saw my mother's car being caught in the blast with my own eyes. The girl next to her died instantly – as for my mother, she had a serious injury in her leg. All this from the shrapnel. If the missile had fallen directly onto the car, it would have been vaporized on the spot. The missile fell close to the car, showering it with shrapnel and spreading an unbelievably strange smell, absolutely foul, it hampered normal breathing. No doubt it was equipped with poisons. The real horror was the sound, the sound of the explosions of the fire belt, as if the earth was splitting in two and screaming in pain. Those explosions are still ringing in my ears, Alhamdulillah. The same thing happened to us a second later. A missile landed extremely close by. I went flying, the car went flying, and inside it were my brother, the driver and his children. I barely understood what was happening until the second missile fell. Everything disappeared. I was looking around but I couldn't see anything. I felt dizzy and heavy-headed; I couldn't see. After a little while, I caught sight of a hand I recognized. It belonged to one of the driver's children. I didn't see his body, just his hand at first, then I saw some of his limbs close to his hand and a few metres away I saw his head lying on his stomach, and his other hand was tangled up with them. Next to that were his guts and more of his limbs . Or perhaps they belonged to someone else? It was like a distorted painting, or a toy put together at random by a child. I looked at him and started laughing. I couldn't do anything but look at him and laugh. I wasn't smiling, I was laughing and I could hear myself laughing. I was looking at my surroundings and laughing. I couldn't see any living creatures, just wreckage, dust and human body parts. I saw I had lost my legs, but I didn't feel any pain – I told you, you don't feel pain from a fresh wound. And the bombing didn't stop, the fire belt hadn't arrived only to depart at the first opportunity. Missiles kept falling, and with every strike I was sent up and flying. During my numerous flights, I saw the corpse of the driver, I saw the bodies of his three sons, they were being pulverized with every strike, hacked to bits. It is hard to describe what was left of them as limbs, the missiles left nothing but shreds. They hacked us to the bone. I was sent flying with every strike, I would land and then go flying again, and I would look at myself, at how I had lost my legs, and I would smile. Why was I smiling? What else could I do? I was sitting calmly, not feeling anything. Perhaps it was the relief of death. A kind-looking man in white came close to me, and he was reciting the Qur'an in a ringing voice:

وَلَا تَحْسَبَنَّ ٱلَّذِينَ قُتِلُوا۟ فِى سَبِيلِ ٱللَّهِ أَمْوَٰتًۢا بَلْ أَحْيَآءٌ عِندَ رَبِّهِمْ يُرْزَقُونَ *

Then he came up to me and asked me in a whisper to choose between life and martyrdom. I said at once, 'I've been in martyrdom for some time.' There, in those final moments, you live in such calm, such serenity, with the Prophets and the Companions and the martyrs and the righteous. The kind-looking man in white was still asking me to choose between martyrdom and life, so I replied, 'I have been in martyrdom for some time.' Then he asked me again, as if he hadn't heard me. After that, while I was seated on the ground on my backside and what remained of my lower limbs, he cleared some debris away from me, took hold of me gently, and laid me down on my back. He stroked my head and murmured something I couldn't understand. I asserted that I wanted martyrdom, then I closed my eyes and his face was the last thing I saw.

I arrived at the hospital, dead. I don't know who took on the burden of moving my body there. Not only was I missing both legs, but my body was also lacerated by several wounds – the half of it that was left, I mean – it contained countless pieces of shrapnel, and it had lost a considerable amount of its flesh and integrity. It was more like the body parts I had seen before my death. The doctors searched for a pulse and a heartbeat in vain. I was dead and they put me in the fridge. Easy enough to put half a body in a nylon bag and throw it into a fridge full of dead people. My friends and my uncle recited the funeral prayer over me, and they cried as they stood in a circle around my body. When my uncle took my hand to

* This comes from Qur'an 3:169.
  'Never think of those martyred in the cause of Allah as dead.
  In fact, they are alive with their Lord, well provided-for.'

235

say goodbye, he screamed and burst into tears. 'He's alive, he's alive!' The doctors told my uncle to calm down and ask God's pardon. 'Astaghfirullah, but he is alive, I swear to God he's alive!' One of them finally believed him and found some signs of life. 'He's alive but dying, he needs six units of blood, perhaps we can save him.' My uncle hurried to bring the units of blood while the doctors were moving me from the mortuary to the operating room. I had spent hours, perhaps, in a plastic bag in a fridge, in the company of corpses. How did that happen? 'We couldn't find your pulse,' the doctor told me, 'and your eyes were open like the dead.' I spent between seven and nine hours in the operating room. Unfortunately, I don't remember anything about it, they told me the details afterwards, after I woke up from the operation. That was also in al-Shifa Hospital, on 26 October, the day after our car was bombed. Little by little, I began to remember what had happened the previous day. I remembered the man in white, I remembered being martyred and closing my eyes on his kind face. I was shivering from a wave of cold that slid into my bones. Then I remembered I'd lost my leg, I had seen it disappear with my own eyes. Odd! I could still feel it. I couldn't move or lift my head to see it for myself, but the doctors and my uncles assured me it was still there. What did I see, in that case? Limbs, my leg disappearing, the angel of death – was all of it a hallu-cination? I hadn't been martyred! It was impossible that everything had just been a nightmare. I could feel my leg, true, but I was certain it had gone flying. My uncle said it was still there, the doctors said it was still there, I could feel it there. Perhaps it was there, then perhaps what happened really was a nightmare. My cousin assured me I walked on it, so it must be there. My remaining half-body underwent several surgeries, it became carved with recesses, and tattooed with stitches, and the doctors were always examining my foot. So it must have still been there. But I was haunted by a strange feeling that everyone was lying to me.

I said to my uncle, 'Uncle, tell me the truth. What happened to my leg?'

'Gone, ammi.'

'Which one do you mean?'

'Both, ammi, both.'

But that wasn't the end of my story in al-Shifa Hospital. I was still in a precarious state. What remained of my lower limbs was decomposing and the doctors had to perform a surgery every time, to clean it out by removing more flesh and bone. They were amputating every time, until there was nothing left for them to amputate. They had reached the very tops of my thighs. That was a very difficult situation. All my family was in hospital. My father was still abroad, my mother was gravely injured, my 3-year-old brother's body was embedded with shrapnel, and so were my sister and my other brother. The doctors wouldn't stop amputating – they wouldn't let me die in peace. I told them, 'I prefer death over seeing you chop another piece off my body.' I prepared myself to die, everyone thought it was inevitable, my condition was so critical. Many things happened – the decomposition stopped, the amputations stopped at the top of my thighs, and I lived. I couldn't grasp what had happened. I remember flashes from before the fire belt: we were in the street, I was in the street and people were walking like normal, I bought some things, I saw our neighbour buying bread that no one ate. We were only a group of civilians, just normal families living a normal life, until what happened happened. An appalling thing. You can't imagine the hideousness of the scene, however I describe it. Bodies and limbs covered every inch. In the blink of an eye, everything was wiped out, homes, shops, warehouses and entire lives vanished. They destroyed everything in Gaza, they destroyed Gaza completely. I want to understand: what was my crime? What was the crime of the children in the car with me? What was the crime of the al-Taj neighbourhood? The area we were in, on Jala Street, its name was al-Taj. It doesn't exist any more. All the people who lived there were doctors, engineers, academics, businessmen.

I heard them, when I was in hospital, whispering that I would die. They were amputating and removing shrapnel and whispering that I was dead. I pretended not to hear them, but I hoped that what they said would come true. I didn't want to live, to heal. I wanted to die, that's all. The pain was tremendous, it didn't respond to painkillers, and what's left of me is as far as can be from a sound human body. All the time, I think of my family, especially of my younger brother. Now he is living alone in Rafah. He lives in a tent, a young boy in a tent, far away from his family. I learned later that he caught hepatitis. Thinking of him kills me.

I see people walking while I am rolling along in a wheelchair and all I can do is ask myself: Why did both legs go? Why didn't at least one of them remain, so I could limp on it?

Why?

'AND THEN THERE ARE ALL THE
THINGS THAT CANNOT BE SPOKEN'

A Note on Translation

One of the central concerns of this book is how to put words around the unspeakability of violence. The translation of experience into language always falls short, but in the case of pain and trauma, the gulf appears insurmountable. These testimonies have been through several translations – into language, into recorded testimony, and then again into English – and I believe we have a moral responsibility to account for how these words have reached these pages. Samar has outlined how she collected and prepared the testimonies; here, I wish to clarify some points about the translation process.

To begin with, I would like to acknowledge and thank Samar Yazbek, her agent Yasmina Jraissati, and the translators into the various languages, who all collaborated to ensure the accounts remain consistent across languages. We are all indebted to Samar for so graciously revisiting a text that must have been immensely difficult for her.

Although I am usually a vehement opponent of footnotes, I have included several throughout the text. I hesitated to do so because I consider footnotes profoundly disrespectful, implying that readers will be too overwhelmed and upset by encountering unfamiliarity to continue without an explanation. Most readers of translated literature are perfectly capable of coping with unexpected learning, and there will be plenty of opportunity to do so in this text. Nevertheless, in the case of these testimonies – whose value is not only literary – I hope the footnotes offer some additional insight. At the risk of condescension, then, I have included brief notes where I personally would find them helpful. They are intended to provide further context for the testimonies, but are not intended as an exhaustive explanation of the history of the genocide.

Readers will no doubt be familiar with the names of Gazan hospitals due to the various sieges and attacks that have taken place over the past two years. The names of these hospitals do not have a consistently agreed translation into English, although I am sure readers will be able to make the necessary connections. There are two clarifications I would like to make, however. Anglophone media variously refers to al-Ahli Arab Baptist Hospital as al-Ahli Hospital, al-Ahli Arab Hospital and so on. The witnesses usually refer to this hospital as 'the Baptist Hospital', which I have respected throughout. I mention this in case readers are not aware that al-Ahli Arab Hospital and the Baptist Hospital are, in fact, one and the same. Similarly, Shuhada al-Aqsa Hospital has been translated as al-Aqsa Martyrs Hospital and al-Aqsa Hospital. For reading ease, the name has been translated here as al-Aqsa Hospital.

Several refugee camps within Gaza – such as Jabalia, al-Maghazi and Nuseirat – appear in the text. Many camps were established in 1948 or in 1967 to house displaced Palestinians and now (or at least, prior to 2023) consist of largely permanent structures. Witnesses sometimes refer to 'al-Maghazi Camp' and at other times simply 'al-Maghazi', implying it is essentially a town of its own. This has been preserved throughout, both to highlight the legacy of these not-so-temporary settlements, and to underscore the liminal experience of Gazans, for whom home and displacement are shifting and unstable. One point to note is that Jabalia Camp is named after Jabalia, a historical town three kilometres away. Some witnesses are from the town and others from the camp, as specified in the chapter headings; in their testimonies, however, the distinction is not always clear. I do not think this particularly impedes understanding, but thought that readers might like to know why the word 'camp' is not always used in the accounts.

With regards to the translation itself, a particular challenge lay in the terminology around how exactly the bombing raids were conducted. English differentiates between missiles and rockets; for those who are unsure of the difference, missiles are propelled and guided, while rockets are propelled but not guided. There is, of course, also vocabulary in Arabic that differentiates between the two, but the word most often used in the testimonies can refer to either. Both have been used on the population of Gaza. In this translation, I have used 'rocket' when referring to Hamas' attack on Israel on 7 October 2023, and 'missile' when referring to Israel's attacks on Gaza. This is because, as far as I can tell, missiles are more commonly used by the Israeli army, particularly when targeting buildings. Like the witnesses themselves, however, I cannot know for certain which was used.

Similarly, on a handful of occasions there is some ambiguity around whether the witnesses are referring to drones or planes. I have exercised my judgement to decide which to use. For obvious reasons, in such cases the ability to clarify this point is limited. If there is a mistake, the responsibility lies with me.

One aspect of the translation which caused me some pain was the decision not to translate the family relationships to their fullest extent. Arabic distinguishes between paternal and maternal relations, and the testimonies are filled with examples of relationship networks which extend into both paternal and maternal families. My editor Tamara Sampey-Jawad and I tried various means of preserving the nuances of these networks, but could not find a workable way to balance this against the readability of the text – and our priority was to ensure the witnesses' stories reached the readers. With regret, I had to give up the attempt. But I wish to underline here that the fabric of Gazan society is woven even more tightly than may come through in the translation, and the ripple effects of death and destruction are felt even more strongly, and even more widely, than can be conveyed easily in English.

In each of the twenty-six testimonies, I have striven to preserve the voice and character as I heard them on the page. This includes instances where phrasing was uncertain, where grammar or articulation was hammered out of shape by the force of trauma, or where narratives were disjointed and disrupted. I appreciate that sometimes this leads to an uncomfortable reading experience, quite apart from the distressing content. Nevertheless, this is the nature of the testimonies. At Samar's suggestion, there have been a handful of minor amendments where details were likely to inhibit understanding. These decisions were taken to preserve clarity, not to obscure detail; for instance, a parent mixes up their children's names (something all parents will relate to), or a witness miscounts the number of dead at that point in their story. While there is certainly an argument for retaining all such inconsistencies, very occasionally we decided that they acted as a barrier to understanding. As to the rest – the contradictions, the unexplained disappearances, the chronological and syntactical turmoil – I trust readers to be able to stay with the witness and to follow the thread of their narrative.

This brings me to my final point. Since the testimonies were gathered, famine has been declared in Gaza. Since this iteration of the war began, 92 per cent of Gaza's houses and 90 per cent of its buildings have been demolished. Ninety-five per cent of the population has been displaced. Two hundred and forty-seven journalists and one thousand seven hundred healthcare workers have been killed. Over 90 per cent of Gaza's schools and universities have been destroyed. Over 90 per cent of agricultural land has been ruined and rendered unusable. Over 80 per cent of the water and sanitation systems have been wiped out. At the two-year anniversary of the outbreak of the current conflict, official figures showed 170,000 wounded and 67,000 dead. The majority of these casualties are civilians. This cannot be justified by the terrible attacks committed by Hamas on 7 October 2023 – nothing could ever justify this devastation. This is a genocide, intended to wipe out Gaza's past, present and future, and has been declared as such by the United Nations.

The twenty-six testimonies here are a brutal read, and they represent an infinitesimal fraction of the human cost of genocide. They offer a way of trying to comprehend the catastrophic destruction hidden behind the statistics. I think about Muhannad Radwan, and the painting he hung up in his room that he was so proud of, and which burned down along with his house. Genocide is too huge for us to comprehend, but these testimonies bring home to us what it feels like to have your humanity called into question. The logistics of displacement when you have nowhere to go. The indignity of not being able to use a bathroom; of not being able to wash your hands; of wearing the same clothes for months on end. The terror of being trapped beneath rubble, not knowing if you will be rescued or if you will slowly die of suffocation. The agony of watching a child die in pain. The shock of having your life and your body ripped apart in seconds. These are not experiences that many of us can relate to directly; all we can do is listen, allow their horror to penetrate, and remember that they are not merely words on a page.

There are over two million stories of this kind in Gaza today. The current ceasefire (such as it is) is fragile, and the prospect of justice looks bleak. What will it take to hold those responsible to account? When will Palestinians be recognized as fully human by those who have it in their power to stop this genocide? I cannot say, but I hope that this book will contribute towards that goal, and I honour Samar for collecting these testimonies, and the witnesses for allowing us to hear their stories.

Leri Price
November 2025

This book has been selected to receive financial assistance from English PEN's 'PEN Translates' programme, supported by Arts Council England. English PEN exists to promote literature and our understanding of it, to uphold writers' freedoms around the world, to campaign against the persecution and imprisonment of writers for stating their views, and to promote the friendly co-operation of writers and the free exchange of ideas.
www.englishpen.org

This book is printed with plant-based inks on materials
certified by the Forest Stewardship Council®. The FSC®
promotes an ecologically, socially and economically
responsible management of the world's forests.
This book has been printed without
the use of plastic-based coatings.

The authorized representative in the EEA
is eucomply OÜ, Pärnu mnt 139b-14,
11317 Tallinn, Estonia.
hello@eucompliancepartner.com
+337 576 90241

Fitzcarraldo Editions
133 Rye Lane
London, SE15 4ST
United Kingdom

ISBN 978-1-80427-241-1

Design by Ray O'Meara
Typeset in Fitzcarraldo
Printed and bound by Pureprint

fitzcarraldoeditions.com

Fitzcarraldo Editions